HE THAT HATH, TO HIM SHALL BE GIVEN: AND HE THAT HATH NOT, FROM HIM SHALL BE TAKEN EVEN THAT WHICH HE HATH.

SUCCESS SERIES

DAG HEWARD-MILLS

Copyright © 2012 Dag Heward-Mills

First published 2012 by Parchment House
1st Printing 2012

E mail Dag Heward-Mills :
evangelist@daghewardmills.org

Find out more about Dag Heward-Mills at:
www.daghewardmills.org

Write to:
Dag Heward-Mills
P.O. Box 114
Korle-Bu
Accra
Ghana

ISBN 13: 978-9988-8500-7-4

Contents

Chapter 1

"He That Hath" and "He That Hath Not"

Is It True?

For he that hath, to him shall be given: and he that hath not, from him shall be taken even that which he hath.

Mark 4:25

It must be true even though it is a strange sounding Scripture! What an unfair sounding Scripture! Why should those who have money be the ones to get even more money? Why should those who have little be the ones to lose even what they have? Why is it that in real life, it is those who have, who get even more? Why is it that things are the exact opposite of what we expect?

Even though this Scripture sounds unfair, it is true for two reasons. *It is true because Jesus said it.* Heaven and earth will pass away but His words will not pass away (Matthew 24:35). The words of Jesus are the most powerful words ever spoken.

The second reason why this Scripture is true is because we see it all around us. Everybody wants more but not everyone gets more. *So who really gets more?*

All of us expect that those who do not have much should be brought up to par. We want everybody to at least have the basics. Yet, both life and history show us that "he that hath" is the one who gets more of everything. Just look around you and see that those who do not have much are losing even the little that they have! We can all see that the words of Jesus are true.

This book is all about this strange sounding Scripture. You will discover that this strange sounding Scripture applies to both physical and spiritual things. Let us look at what "he that hath" means.

"He That Hath" Physical Things

1.   "He that hath" money, houses and cars shall have more money, more houses and more cars.

Rich people ("he that hath") get richer and never seem to lack anything whilst the poor get poorer every day. Africa, the poorest continent in the world is the only part of the world that has consistently become poorer over the last thirty years.

America and Europe, which are already rich, have become wealthier and increased their gold reserves, their fortunes and their properties. Africa on the other hand, which needs more infrastructure, has destroyed its little infrastructure through civil wars and tribal conflicts.

It is clear that a person who has built a house is more likely to build more houses. A person who has not built a house is less likely to build a house in the future. A person who does not have a house is more likely to lose his present accommodation. A person who has not built a house is more likely to be ejected by his landlord.

People who have cars are more likely to own more cars in the future. Poor people who do not own cars but are always riding in buses and taxies are more likely to be riding in buses and taxis in the years to come.

2. "He that hath" a job shall have even more job offers.

The one who has a job is more likely to get more jobs. If you are a chef at the Golden Tulip Hotel you are likely to be approached by the new Sheraton Hotel to be its chef. Unfortunately, the person who has just finished a chef's course at the local catering school is less likely to be offered the job at the new Sheraton Hotel. "He that hath" a job is more likely to have another job. A person working as a Treasurer of a bank is more likely to be approached by another bank with an offer of an even better job. Sadly, a person who has earned two degrees at the university is less likely to be approached by the bank. This person will have to diligently seek for a job and be turned away many times.

3. "He that hath" a child shall have even more children.

People who have children more easily give birth to the next child. It is common to find existing mothers being unhappy because they have become pregnant. Such people already have a number of children. Sadly, those who don't have any children at all struggle to have even one. It is a sad paradox but it is a reality in our world.

4.   "He that hath" political power shall have more political power.

Families that have political power are more likely to have more political power. You may ask, "Why should the Bush family have two American presidents?" "Why should the Kennedy family have two presidents?"

You may want some other family to have some famous politicians or presidents coming out of them. But it is more likely that there will be more presidents coming out of the already famous family.

5.   "He that hath" education shall have more education.

It is more likely that a family of lawyers and doctors will give birth to more lawyers and doctors. It is unlikely that a family of illiterates and villagers will give birth to people who will become lawyers, doctors and scientists.

So, the Scripture is fulfilled again. He that has educated people in his family gets even more educated people in his family. He that does not have educated people in his family seems to lose even that which he has.

6.   "He that hath" friends in high places shall have even more friends.

Someone who knows important people is likely to know even more important people as the years go by. A villager or an impoverished illiterate who does not know any engineer, doctor or lawyer is less likely to know an important person by next year. Actually because of his poverty, people are likely to lose interest in him and his friends are likely to become fewer.

7.   He that is famous shall become even more famous.

Someone who is famous is likely to become even more famous if he continues to do the things he is doing. An unknown person in the village is not likely to become famous in the coming year.

"He That Hath" Spiritual Things

1. **"He that hath" the knowledge of God is more likely to increase in this knowledge.** He is likely to increase in the knowledge and fear of God. Such people who are anointed are likely to become even more anointed in the coming years.

2. **The evangelist that has won many souls is likely to win more souls in the coming year.** He is likely to have even bigger crusades whiles the evangelist who has very small crowds is likely to experience diminishing attendance to his small crusades. The young man in the church who has only won one soul in his entire Christian life is not likely to win any souls this year.

3. **The pastor that has a big church is likely to have an even bigger church in the coming year.** A pastor who has a big church is more likely to have a bigger church. A small church is more likely to become smaller. A small

church is more likely to lose members and to close down than a big church.

4. **The anointed servant of God seems to be becoming more gifted and anointed.** They seem to reach out further and do more exploits for the Lord. People who are not gifted seem to become even less attractive. They tend to become even more unanointed.

5. **Pastors who have church buildings seem to build even more buildings.** Those who do not have a home for their churches seem to be threatened with ejection from their rented premises. Church members seem to flock to the bigger churches from the smaller churches, depleting the already small size of the small congregations.

6. **Churches which have a high income are more likely to have a high income in the coming year.** Churches with a low income are likely to lose members and lose income in the coming year.

7. **Ministers of the Gospel who have trained many up and coming leaders are likely to train even more.** People who have never trained leaders are less likely to ever have a successor.

Why Is It So?

Why is it that Jesus' statement, "whoever has will be given more" is so true?

Why "He That Hath" Will Have More

Those who "have" did certain things that enabled them to come by what they had. Usually those who "have" *continue to practise the same principles of increase.*

Why "He That Hath Not" Will Lose Even What He Has

Take therefore the talent from him, and give *it* unto him which hath ten talents.

Matthew 25:28

Those who do not have much, do not practise certain principles or follow certain ideals that lead to riches. Usually, those who do not have continue and persist in the bad principles and ideas that have led them to their existing state of poverty. This causes their poverty to deepen and their problems become even more complicated.

A quick glance at African countries and economies will reveal an even more complicated and deep-rooted poverty than existed fifty years ago. If it would have taken a miracle to lift Africa out of its colonial poverty, it will now take a thousand more miracles to lift Africa out of where it is. This is because the difficulties and challenges of Africa have grown, multiplied and developed into complex problems which have very complex solutions.

A ministry that is struggling, deeply in crisis, difficulties and poverty often has problems that go beyond the natural eye. Often, they have deep-seated, complicated and long-standing problems. These problems are often *complications of complicated problems*. This is why Jesus said: He that has will be given more and he that does not have will lose what he even has.

What Must We Do?

What must we do now? We must honestly identify the causes of the inequalities that exist in our world – both spiritually and financially. We must identify the little differences that make the big differences that we see. We must apply ourselves to the lessons that we learn from "he that hath". There is no quick fix to going from poverty to riches.

This is not a book on prosperity. There is nothing wrong with books on prosperity. I believe in prosperity. But this is a book that goes further to understand the mystical words of Jesus: "he that hath" to him more shall be given and "he that hath not", even what he has shall be taken away from him. If you apply the principles of this book you will become "he that hath".

Amazingly, studies done by secular researchers confirm the truths of Jesus' words. A closer look at the things which secular people have discovered are very helpful in understanding why "he that hath" receiveth even more and "he that hath not" loses even that which he has.

Jesus' words are so profound. Even without research, Jesus' words are the words that explain what has given rise to the "haves" and the "have nots" of this world.

Do not despise the knowledge and wisdom that is revealed in this book. Take it seriously because the Spirit of God is the Spirit of knowledge.

Indeed, there is no wisdom like the wisdom of Jesus and there are no words like His words. Heaven and earth will pass away but you will discover that those who "have" receive even more and those who do not "have" lose even the little that they have.

Chapter 2

"He That Hath" Will Get Even More Because He Has Positive Traits and Attitudes

And beside this, giving all diligence, add to your faith virtue; and to virtue knowledge;

And to knowledge temperance; and to temperance patience; and to patience godliness;

And to godliness brotherly kindness; and to brotherly kindness charity.

For IF THESE THINGS BE IN YOU, AND ABOUND, they make *you that YE SHALL* NEITHER *BE* BARREN NOR UNFRUITFUL in the knowledge of our Lord Jesus Christ.

2 Peter 1:5-8

The Scripture above shows us that if you have certain "things" in you, you will not be barren, unfruitful or unproductive. The "things" that Peter is referring to are positive traits like diligence, faith, virtue, temperance etc. It is these positive traits in a person's character that lead to fruitfulness or productivity.

It is positive traits in someone's personality that cause him to break out of the unfruitful, unproductive and non-prosperous zones. Barrenness speaks of an arid landscape with very little productivity. The dry and barren fields of "he that hath not" testify of the lack of certain positive traits in that individual. What are the positive traits in an individual that make him into "he that hath?" That is what this chapter is about. There are nine important positive traits associated with fruitfulness, productivity and abundance.

These positive traits are identified in the Word of God and in the passage above. They are the personal traits that will make anyone rich. These personal traits must be identified, encouraged and developed in you so that you can become "he that hath." The Bible teaches us that once these positive traits are present there will be no unfruitfulness, barrenness or poverty.

The positive traits are *diligence, faith, virtue, knowledge, temperance, patience, godliness, brotherly love* and *charity*. Because these traits are so important you must know a few things about each of them and understand how they work.

POSITIVE TRAIT: DILIGENCE

Diligence defined: Diligence is the *persistent and relentless effort* by an individual to solve a problem, to overcome difficulties and to accomplish great things.

Four Things You Should Know about Diligence

1.   Diligence is the personal trait that makes a person rich.

Almost every rich person is a diligent person.

He becometh poor that dealeth with a slack hand: but the hand of THE DILIGENT MAKETH RICH.

                                                            Proverbs 10:4

2.   Diligence is the personal trait that makes a person a leader. Most leaders are rich and prosperous because they are ahead of everyone they lead.

The hand of the DILIGENT SHALL BEAR RULE: but the slothful shall be under tribute.

                                                            Proverbs 12:24

3.   Diligence is the personal trait that makes a person have ideas that lead to abundance and wealth.

The THOUGHTS OF THE DILIGENT TEND ONLY TO PLENTEOUSNESS; but of every one that is hasty only to want.

                                                            Proverbs 21:5

4.   Diligence is the personal trait that leads to promotion.

Seest thou a man diligent in his business? HE SHALL STAND BEFORE KINGS; he shall not stand before mean men.

Proverbs 22:29

In history, diligence is what has created wealthy, successful people. A close look at leaders, millionaires and men of abundance will often reveal lots of diligence and hard work. The story of how *KFC* was established is a classic case of the importance of diligence.

How Diligence Created the World-Famous Kentucky Fried Chicken Business

When Colonel Harland Sanders retired at the age of 65, he had little to show for himself, except an old Caddie roadster, a $105 monthly pension check, and a recipe for chicken.

Knowing he couldn't live on his pension, he took his chicken recipe in hand, got behind the wheel of his van, and set out to make his fortune. His first plan was to sell his chicken recipe to restaurant owners, who would in turn give him a residual for every piece of chicken they sold - 5 cents per chicken. The first restaurateur he called on turned him down.

So did the second.

So did the third.

So did the next one thousand.

In fact, the first 1008 sales calls Colonel Sanders made ended in rejection. Still, he continued to call on owners as he travelled across the USA, sleeping in his car to save money. *Prospect number 1009 gave him his first "yes."* Here you may understand the definition of diligence better: *The persistent and relentless effort by an individual to solve a problem, to overcome difficulties and to accomplish great things.*

After two years of making daily sales he had signed up a total of five restaurants. Still the Colonel pressed on, knowing that he had a great chicken recipe and that someday the idea would catch on.

Of course, you know how the story ends. The idea did catch on. By 1963 the Colonel had 600 restaurants across the country selling his secret recipe of Kentucky Fried Chicken (with 11 herbs and spices).

In 1964 he was bought out by future Kentucky governor John Brown. Even though the sale made him a multi-millionaire, he continued to represent and promote KFC until his death in 1990.

Colonel Sanders' story teaches an important lesson: it is never too late to decide to never give up. Earlier in his life the Colonel was involved in other business ventures - but they weren't successful. He had a gas station in the 30's, a restaurant in the 40's, and he gave up on both of them. At the age of 65, however, Harland Sanders decided his chicken idea was the right idea, and he refused to give up, even in spite of repeated rejection.

He knew that if he kept on knocking on doors, eventually someone would say "yes." This is how Jesus has commanded us to approach life. Diligence! Jesus said, "Ask and it will be given to you; seek and you will find; knock and the door will be opened to you" (Luke 11:9). We must be relentless and inexorable in our mission.

The Diligence of Abraham Lincoln

Abraham Lincoln, a famous president of USA, is another good example of an inexorable, never-give-up/never-give-in man of diligence. In spite of repeated failure and difficulties, he persisted in his political mission until he was successful. Notice how his numerous defeats did not deter him. He persisted and his relentless efforts paid off in the end.

He failed in business in 1831,

He was defeated for legislature in 1832,

He experienced a second failure in business in 1833,

He suffered nervous breakdown in 1836,

He was defeated for Speaker in 1838,

He was defeated for Elector in 1840,

He was defeated for Congress in 1843,

He was defeated for Congress in 1848,

He was defeated for Senate in 1855,

He was defeated for Vice-President in 1856,

He was defeated for Senate in 1858,

He was finally elected President in 1860.

Perhaps now, you will understand why a person with the positive trait of diligence is usually a successful person. A diligent person will surely become "he that hath".

POSITIVE TRAIT: FAITH

Faith defined: *Faith is a firm belief in something for which there is no proof. It is also a belief in God.*

Six Things You Should Know about Faith

1. **Faith is the personal trait that will cause you to overcome big problems and obstacles. "For verily I say unto you, that whosoever shall say unto this MOUNTAIN, be thou removed, and be thou cast into the sea; and shall not doubt in his heart, but shall believe that those things which he saith shall come to pass; he shall have whatsoever he saith" (Mark 11:23).**

   People who have faith are able to move mountains. A mountain is a big problem. To move mountains around and become "he that hath" you will need the positive trait of faith. Great achievements are usually great victories over insurmountable challenges.

2. **Faith is the personal trait that causes an individual to have a good report. "For by it the elders obtained a good report" (Hebrews 11:2).**

   To have a good report that you are experiencing abundance, you need to be a little wiser than the neighbourhood monkey. You will need to see the correlation between positive traits and prosperity. Bible teaches us that good reports were given to men of faith. Good things are usually said about positive faith-filled people who believed in a vision before it became a reality. You always remember the people who believed in you before things worked out. There are people who come along but never believe in you or your vision. Such

15

people will not have a good report. A good report is for those who believe when there is nothing to see.

3. **Faith is the personal trait that makes a person victorious. "For whatsoever is born of God overcometh the world: and this is the victory that overcometh the world, even our faith" (1 John 5:4).**

Victory is given to men of faith. Without faith you will never be victorious and become "he that hath."   The victory that you need will be provided - through your faith in God.

4. **Faith is the personal trait that makes a person a visionary. "By faith he forsook Egypt, not fearing the wrath of the king: for he endured as SEEING HIM WHO IS INVISIBLE" (Hebrews 11:27).**

A visionary is someone who can see the future. He can see how it is going to work out.

Faith is the evidence of things not seen. Without faith you cannot visualize or imagine a good outcome and a good future. Without faith you will be full of complaints, murmuring and grumblings. You will never see the great possibilities of what God can do for you. All your calculations will be based on "here and now" because you cannot see the invisible. Moses was a great man of faith. He   endured and was successful because he saw *the invisible.*

5. **Faith is the personal trait that makes a person no longer a fool. "The fool hath said in his heart, There is no God..." (Psalm 14:1).**

A fool says there is no God. Having faith in God catapults you out of foolishness into wisdom.

6. **Faith is the personal trait that pleases God the most. "But without faith it is impossible to please him..." (Hebrews 11:6).**

   Somehow, without faith it is impossible to make God happy with you. You need to be positive, you need to think correctly and you need to expect positive things if you are to please God.

POSITIVE TRAIT: VIRTUE

Virtue defined: *Virtue is the quality of doing what is good and right and avoiding wrong.*

There are seven known cardinal virtues. Four of them are natural virtues and three of them are theological virtues. The four natural virtues are justice, prudence, temperance and fortitude. The three spiritual virtues are faith, hope and love.

To live a life of doing what is right and avoiding what is wrong, you need to deploy justice, prudence, temperance, fortitude, faith, hope and love. Fortitude speaks of the strength of mind that enables one to endure adversity.

Four Things You Must Know about Virtue (Goodness)

1. **Virtue is a personal positive trait that makes you abhor evil.** A virtuous person is full of goodness, righteousness and has strong morals.

   ...Abhor that which is evil; cleave to that which is GOOD.

   Romans 12:9

2. **Virtue (goodness) is the personal trait that prevents a person from randomly following after the opposite sex.** Ruth was a virtuous woman. She refused to follow after young men, whether poor or rich. She was concerned about doing what is right. Many people are not rich because they follow after the opposite sex and are destroyed by many enchantments, pleasures and deceptions.

And he said, Blessed be thou of the Lord, my daughter: for thou hast shewed more kindness in the latter end than at the beginning, inasmuch as THOU FOLLOWEDST NOT YOUNG MEN, whether poor or rich.

And now, my daughter, fear not; I will do to thee all that thou requirest: for all the city of my people doth know that THOU ART A VIRTUOUS WOMAN.

Ruth 3:10-11

3. **Virtue (goodness) is the personal trait that makes a person genuinely helpful.** Virtue (goodness) is the personal trait that makes you do good to people and not evil. A virtuous woman does good to her husband and not evil. Without virtue a beautiful woman is a useless object moving around.

The Bible says beauty is vain. It is only when virtue comes into a female that she does good to a man. Many women do evil to their men because they lack virtue. Virtue is very different from beauty. Beauty is useless but virtue is valuable. When a person does good to someone he will be rewarded. Rewards for doing good and not evil to a person are what make a person become "he that hath."

Who can find a VIRTUOUS WOMAN? for her price
is far above rubies… SHE WILL DO HIM GOOD and
not evil all the days of her life.

Proverbs 31:10

4. **Virtue (goodness) is the personal trait that makes a
    person hardworking, energetic and enterprising.** The
    only person described as virtuous in the Bible is the
    virtuous woman of Proverbs 31. Her main characteristics
    were hard work and lots of industrious activity. She
    would rise up early, she would gird up her loins and she
    would make things happen for the whole household.

This cannot be said of many beautiful women whose
principal achievement is to dress up and make themselves
look more and more artificial. Their beauty is a façade
and a cover up for their emptiness. Their enhanced
appearance is a sign of the level of deception you must
expect from such non-virtuous characters.

You will have the greatest shocks when you are married to
someone who has no virtue. You will be met by laziness,
inaction and inactivity. You will also be met by the poor
provision of food, sex and anything that doesn't happen in
the public eye. You will notice how the virtuous woman
of Proverbs 31 goes around working hard and making
everyone in her household have what they need. She is
more concerned about meeting the needs of her household
than impressing outsiders.

A virtuous woman is full of truth, reality and genuineness.

The story below teaches us the importance of doing what
is good and right. Doing what is good and right will
always lead to abundance. Virtue is a positive trait that
will turn you into "he that hath".

Ching Chong Chang

An emperor in the Far East was growing old and knew it was time to choose his successor. Instead of choosing one of his assistants or his children, he decided something different. He called young people in the kingdom together one day. He said, "It is time for me to step down and choose the next emperor. I have decided to choose one of you."

The kids were shocked! But the emperor continued, "I am going to give each one of you a seed today. One very special seed! I want you to plant the seed, water it and come back here after one year from today with what you have grown from this one seed. I will then judge the plants that you bring, and the one I choose will be the next emperor!"

One boy named Ching Chong Chang was there that day and he, like the others, received a seed. He went home and excitedly told his mother the story. She helped him get a pot and planting soil, and he planted the seed and watered it carefully. Every day he would water it and watch to see if it had grown. After about three weeks, some of the other youths began to talk about their seeds and the plants that were beginning to grow. Ching Chong Chang kept checking his seed, but nothing ever grew. 3 weeks, 4 weeks, 5 weeks went by. Still nothing. By now, others were talking about their plants but Ching Chong Chang didn't have a plant, and he felt like a failure. Six months went by, still nothing in Ching Chong Chang's pot. He just knew he had killed his seed.

Everyone else had trees and tall plants, but he had nothing. Ching Chong Chang didn't say anything to his friends, however. He just kept waiting for his seed to grow.

A year finally went by and all the youths of the kingdom brought their plants to the emperor for inspection. Ching Chong Chang told his mother that he wasn't going to take an empty pot. But his mother told him to be honest about what happened. Ching Chong Chang knew his mother was right so he took his empty pot to the palace. When Ching Chong Chang arrived, he was amazed at the variety of plants grown by the other youths. They were beautiful in all shapes and sizes. Ching Chong Chang put his empty pot on the floor and many of the other youths laughed at him. A few felt sorry for him and just said, "Hey nice try."

When the emperor arrived, he surveyed the room and greeted the young people. Ching Chong Chang just tried to hide in the back. "What great plants, trees and flowers you have grown," said the emperor. "Today, one of you will be appointed the next emperor!" All of a sudden, the emperor spotted Ching Chong Chang at the back of the room with his empty pot. He ordered his guards to bring him to the front. Ching Chong Chang was terrified. "The emperor knows I'm a failure! Maybe he will have me killed!"

When Ching Chong Chang got to the front, the Emperor asked his name. "My name is Ching Chong Chang," he replied. All the kids were laughing and making fun of him. The emperor asked everyone to quiet down. He looked at Ching Chong Chang, and then announced to the crowd, "Behold your new emperor! His name is Ching Chong Chang!" Ching Chong Chang couldn't believe it.

Ching Chong Chang couldn't even grow his seed. How could he be the new emperor? Then the emperor said, "One year ago today, I gave everyone here a seed. I told you to take the seed, plant it, water it, and bring it back to me today. *But I gave you all boiled seeds*, which would not grow. All of you, except Ching Chong Chang, have brought me trees and plants and flowers. When you found that the seed would not grow, you substituted another seed for the one I gave you. Ching Chong Chang was the only one with the courage and honesty to bring me a pot with my seed in it. Therefore, he is the one who will be the new emperor!"

Indeed, the young man exhibited virtue which earned him the crown. Courage, honesty and truthfulness are indeed powerful keys to make you into "he that hath."

POSITIVE TRAIT: KNOWLEDGE

Knowledge defined: *Knowledge is the condition in which you are aware of facts and realities that are true, important and relevant.*

Knowledge is very important and the absence of knowledge (ignorance) correlates well with almost every known evil on earth. The more educated a nation is, and the more knowledge it has, the richer it is. The life expectancy of every group is related to the amount of knowledge they have.

The importance of knowledge and its value in having more is easily illustrated by the distribution of poverty and misery in the earth. If you want to become "he that hath" you will need to love knowledge and wisdom and acquire them with all your heart.

Six Things You Should Know about Knowledge

1.   Knowledge is a very valuable personal positive trait. Knowledge is so valuable that it is called a treasure.

In whom are hid all the TREASURES of wisdom and KNOWLEDGE.

Colossians 2:3

2.   Knowledge is the personal trait that causes you to live a good and humble life.

WHO IS a wise man and ENDUED WITH KNOWLEDGE among you? let him shew out of a good conversation HIS WORKS WITH MEEKNESS of wisdom.

James 3:13

3.   Knowledge is the personal trait that causes you to be filled with grace and peace.

GRACE AND PEACE be multiplied unto you THROUGH THE KNOWLEDGE of God, and of Jesus our Lord,

2 Peter 1:2

4.   Knowledge is the personal trait that causes you to acquire all things that pertain to life and godliness.

According as his divine power hath GIVEN UNTO US ALL THINGS that pertain unto life and godliness,

THROUGH THE KNOWLEDGE of him that hath called us to glory and virtue:

2 Peter 1:3

5.   Knowledge is a personal trait that causes you to escape the corruption of this world.

For if after they have ESCAPED THE POLLUTIONS OF THE WORLD THROUGH THE KNOWLEDGE of the Lord and Saviour Jesus Christ, they are again entangled therein, and overcome, the latter end is worse with them than the beginning.

2 Peter 2:20

6.   Knowledge is a personal trait that allows you to live with weaker personalities.

Likewise, ye husbands, DWELL WITH THEM ACCORDING TO KNOWLEDGE, giving honour unto the wife, as unto the weaker vessel, and as being heirs together of the grace of life; that your prayers be not hindered.

1 Peter 3:7

Knowledge will change your attitude to people. Knowledge will increase your understanding of different situations and help you to manage people better until you live in prosperity.

The Man and the Hawk

A man had a hawk for his pet. The pet used to help him when he went hunting. One day as they went hunting the man became very thirsty because they had been walking for a long

24

time. Just then the man saw a small stream of water dripping down a rock. He was so excited about the fresh cool water that was coming out of the rock. He took out his cup and held it out to receive the water coming from the rock above. Just as he was about to lift the cup to his lips, his hawk pet, in a quick swoop kicked his cup, pouring out all the water.

To his amazement his pet swooped down and kicked the cup each time he was about to drink some water. After the third swoop, he angrily pulled out his sword and slashed at the hawk.

He then picked up his pet hawk which lay dying in a pool of blood. But it suddenly occurred to him that his hawk must have known something that he didn't. There must have been some reason why the hawk didn't want him to drink the water. He decided to climb up the rock to see for himself. And what did he see?

There, on the top of the mountain lay a dead poisonous snake in a pool of water. It was this poisonous water that was dripping slowly down the mountain and into his cup. His pet had knowledge that he did not have. His lack of knowledge made him walk into danger. His lack of knowledge made him attack his own helper. His lack of knowledge made him kill his friend. His lack of knowledge made him destroy what he needed most.

Dear friend, knowledge is a very important positive trait that will transform your life. A lack of knowledge leads to a loss of the very things that you need.

POSITIVE TRAIT: TEMPERANCE

Temperance defined: *Temperance is the trait of avoiding excesses and living in moderation.*

Seven Things You Should Know about Temperance

1. **Temperance is a personal trait that makes you receive the highest rewards**. People who are moderate in all things are self-disciplined and are able to achieve great things in their lives.

   And EVERY MAN THAT STRIVETH FOR THE MASTERY IS TEMPERATE in all things. Now they do it to obtain a corruptible crown; but we an incorruptible.

   1 Corinthians 9:25

2. **Temperance is a personal trait that makes people accept and enjoy privileges at the right time.** A person with the positive trait of temperance will not use his privileges at the least opportunity but will wait until the most appropriate season. This cannot be said of primitive leaders who scramble for privileges from the very first day they enter office.

   BLESSED ART THOU, O LAND, WHEN thy king is the son of nobles, and THY PRINCES EAT IN DUE SEASON, for strength, and not for drunkenness!

   Ecclesiastes 10:17

3. **Temperance is a personal trait that makes people accept privileges only because it makes them stronger.**

   Blessed art thou, O land when thy king is the son of nobles, and THY PRINCES EAT in due season, FOR STRENGTH, and not for drunkenness!

   Ecclesiastes 10:17

4. **Temperance is a personal trait that makes you react to provocation moderately and cautiously.** People without temperance tend to react inappropriately. Temperance turns a person into a man of great understanding.

    HE THAT IS SLOW TO WRATH IS OF GREAT UNDERSTANDING: but he that is hasty of spirit exalteth folly.

    Proverbs 14:29

5. **Temperance is a personal trait that makes a leader not misuse his great authority and power.** When a leader misuses his great authority and power he becomes an oppressor and a murderer. Leadership often comes with great authority and the world is full of examples of people who have misused their great authority and privileges. Temperance is the positive trait that prevents a leader from becoming oppressive.

    The prince that wanteth understanding is also a great oppressor...

    Proverbs 28:16

6. **Temperance is a personal trait that causes a leader to be moderate in acquiring personal wealth.**

    ... he that hateth covetousness shall prolong his days.

    Proverbs 28:16

7. **Temperance is a personal trait that comes from the long-term influence of the Holy Spirit.**

    But the FRUIT of the SPIRIT is love, joy, peace, longsuffering, gentleness, goodness, faith, meekness, TEMPERANCE: against such there is no law.

    Galatians 5:22-23

POSITIVE TRAIT: PATIENCE

Patience defined: *Patience is the good-natured tolerance of delay or incompetence.* To be patient is to be steadfast despite opposition, difficulty or adversity. A patient person bears pains and trials without complaint.

Three Things You Should Know about Patience

1. **Patience is the personal trait that will cause you to bear fruit.** To be productive you need to be patient for things to grow until the day of harvest. Patience is a very important trait for productivity and prosperity. Because of a lack of patience people jump out of a good thing, thinking they can get to the top faster.

   But that on the good ground are they, which in an honest and good heart, having heard the word, keep it, and BRING FORTH FRUIT WITH PATIENCE.

   Luke 8:15

2. **Patience is the personal trait that makes you inherit good things.** "Rest in the Lord and wait patiently for him." These are the words of the psalmist. "Fret not thyself because of him who prospereth in his way...for evil doers shall be cut off: but those that wait upon the Lord, they shall inherit the earth" (Psalm 37:7, 9).

   That ye be not slothful, but followers of them who THROUGH faith and PATIENCE INHERIT the promises.

   Hebrews 6:12

3. **Patience is the personal trait that will cause you to be approved.** You will be approved because you were able

28

to wait for your day of promotion. The ability to wait faithfully is always rewarded with promotion. Pastors of big churches are all people who have stayed in one place for many years. Wait patiently and you will become someone who can be described as "he that hath."

But in all things APPROVING OURSELVES AS THE MINISTERS OF GOD, IN MUCH PATIENCE, in afflictions, in necessities, in distresses,

2 Corinthians 6:4

The Golden Eggs

One day, a farmer's hen suddenly began laying golden eggs. One morning, upon going to the nest of his chickens he found a glittering yellow and glowing egg. When he took it up it was as heavy as lead and he was going to throw it away because he thought a trick had been played upon him. But he took it home on second thoughts. He soon found to his delight that it was a pure golden egg. Every morning the same thing occurred and he soon became rich by selling his golden eggs.

As he grew rich he began to calculate how much money he would have at the end of the year when his chicken would have laid over three hundred eggs. He thought to himself, "I can't wait for this chicken to lay an egg a day. It is too slow for me. If I could get all the eggs out of its stomach in one go, I would be very rich and could invest now in buildings and other businesses."

He thought to himself, "I would no longer need to be a farmer. I could go into business."

Then he had a brainwave and said to himself, "If I cut open the chicken's stomach I could take out all the three hundred eggs and become a millionaire immediately. I will no longer have to prosper in bits and pieces as I am doing now." The next day he cut open the chicken's stomach and to his amazement there were no eggs. His impatience cost him his fortune. He could not wait for the golden eggs to be laid every day. He had to have it now.

This is the power of impatience. It is the power that destroys your own fruits and your own rewards. The power of impatience contains the power of self destruction.

POSTIVE TRAIT: GODLINESS

Godliness defined: Godliness is the quality of being like God. God has many attributes: God is love, God is light and God is His Word. When you become godly you are filled with these positive traits and become like God in your behaviour and character.

Four Things You Should Know about Godliness

1. **Godliness is the personal trait in a person that makes him pray at the right time.** Most people pray in time of trouble but a godly person will pray at a time when God can be found. A person who prays will be helped by God. When you meet someone who prays you will discover that he has one of the most important positive traits a human being can have. The most successful pastors that I know have the positive trait being godly and praying at a time when God can be found.

   For this shall EVERY ONE THAT IS GODLY PRAY unto thee in a time when thou mayest be found: surely in the floods of great waters they shall not come nigh unto him.

Psalm 32:6

2. **Godliness is a positive personal trait that will set you apart.** A godly person will always be distinguished and set apart because of the God factor in his life. Do you want God to set you apart? Do you want to be distinguished amongst your brethren? Then be a godly person.

But know that the Lord hath SET APART HIM THAT IS GODLY for himself: the Lord will hear when I call unto him.

Psalm 4:3

3. **Godliness is a positive trait that affects all aspects of your life.** Godliness is pervasive in its influence over your life. It affects every decision and every step you ever make. Godliness will change you into a successful person because God is mighty and all-powerful.

For bodily exercise profiteth little: but GODLINESS IS PROFITABLE UNTO ALL THINGS, having promise of the life that now is, and of that which is to come.

1 Timothy 4:8

4. **Godliness is a positive trait that makes you unlike man.** When you are godly your emotions are unlike man's emotions. Even the most basic emotions are affected and turned into a godly version of human emotions. You will have godly jealousy (2 Corinthians 11:2), godly sorrow (2 Corinthians 7:10) and godly fear

(Hebrews 12:28). You will be unlike man who has debilitating weaknesses like lying and unfaithfulness (Number 23:19).

POSITIVE TRAIT: BROTHERLY LOVE

Brotherly Love defined: Brotherly Love is the love that a person has for a brother. It is the strong affection for another that rises out of kinship and personal relationships. Brotherly love shows concern for others. When something affects your brother it must affect you. That is brotherly love.

Three Things You Should Know about Brotherly Love

1. **The personal trait of brotherly love humbly puts others before you.** This is humility; and before honour is humility.

   Be kindly affectioned one to another with BROTHERLY LOVE; IN HONOUR PREFERRING one another;

   Romans 12:10

2. **The personal trait of brotherly love is needed to prevent strife between close relations.**

   And Abram said unto Lot, LET THERE BE NO STRIFE, I pray thee, between me and thee, and between my herdmen and thy herdmen; FOR WE BE BRETHREN.

   Genesis 13:8

3. **The personal trait of brotherly love causes you to sacrifice yourself for others.** Brotherly love causes you to lay down your love for the brethren. People who are sacrificial and lay down themselves for others are often productive.

Hereby perceive we the love of God, because he laid down his life for us: and we ought to LAY DOWN OUR LIVES FOR THE BRETHREN.

1 John 3:16

The Mouse, the Chicken, the Pig and the Cow

In this story, the chicken, the pig and the cow did not have brotherly love for their fellow farm animals and paid a high price for it.

One day, the farm mouse looked through the crack in the wall to see the farmer and his wife open a package. What food might this contain?" the mouse wondered. He was devastated to discover it was a mousetrap. Retreating to the farmyard, the mouse proclaimed the warning.

He rushed to the chicken and told him, "There is a mousetrap in the house! There is a mousetrap in the house!"

The chicken clucked and scratched, raised her head and said, "Mr. Mouse, what is the meaning of this frenzied outburst? You are talking too much and disturbing our children. We have a job to do on this farm. Honestly, I cannot be bothered by a mousetrap. A mousetrap is no reason for you to disturb the neighbourhood.

The mouse turned to the pig and told him, "There is a mousetrap in the house! There is a mousetrap in the house!" The pig sympathized, but said, "I am so very sorry, Mr. Mouse, but there is nothing anyone can do about it. If you were to eat more and grow bigger you would not be worried about mousetraps. Anyway, be assured that you are in my prayers."

The mouse then turned to the cow and said, "There is a mousetrap in the house! There is a mousetrap in the house!" The cow said, "Mr. Mouse, pull yourself together! I can give you some advice. Just be careful when you are walking around and everything will be alright. A mousetrap is not a dangerous thing!"

So, the mouse returned to the house, head down and dejected, to face the farmer's mousetrap alone. None of the other animals had understood his dilemma. None of them really cared.

That very night a sound was heard throughout the house - like the sound of a mousetrap catching its prey. The farmer's wife rushed to see what was caught. In the darkness, she did not see it was a venomous snake whose tail the trap had caught. The snake lunged out and bit the farmer's wife. The farmer rushed her to the hospital where she was treated for snakebite. After three days in the hospital, the farmer's wife returned home but with a persisting fever. Everyone knew that the treatment for fever was *fresh chicken soup*. The farmer took a decision to give his wife the fresh chicken soup that she needed. He caught the chicken, killed it and made fresh soup for his wife.

But his wife's sickness continued, so friends and neighbours came to sit with her around the clock. To feed them, the farmer decided to serve the guests with pork chops, pork stew, spare ribs and some bacon and sausages. The pig was quickly summoned, slaughtered and converted into these delicacies. In spite of the special treatment and care that the farmer's wife received, she did not get any better and eventually died.

So many people came for her funeral. The farmer was not expecting so many guests and had to suddenly cater for hundreds of funeral mourners. His relatives asked him to serve the guests with beef stew, steak, khebab and some meatballs. They said to him, "You will be able to buy another cow after the funeral."

Under pressure from his family, he took the decision to slaughter his cow and serve his funeral guests.

The mouse looked upon it all from his crack in the wall with great sadness. Indeed, the chicken, the pig and the cow never thought that the arrival of the mousetrap to the farm would one day affect them all.

When you have brotherly love you quickly recognize that your brother's problem is actually your problem. It takes wisdom and maturity to realize how another person's problem will eventually come to you.

CHARITY

Charity defined: *Charity is the unselfish, loyal and benevolent concern for the good of another.* It is the selfless love of one person for another. Most people love others when they have a good reason to do so. But God loves us with agape love (charity) even though there is no good reason to do so. Somehow, people who have charity prosper and receive even more blessings from the Lord. If you only do good because you think of a reward, you do not have charity.

Three Things You Should Know about Charity

1. **Charity is the personal trait that leads to unity.** With unity almost everything is possible. Your visions and dreams are achievable when you have the love of God. Through love you will be united and will be able to achieve great things.

   And above all these things put on CHARITY, WHICH IS THE BOND of perfectness.

   Colossians 3:14

2. **Charity is the personal trait that causes you never to fail.** Your ministry will never fail, your church will never fail, and your marriage will never fail if you have the love of God. Love never fails! This is the best positive trait you could desire for yourself. It is the element that guarantees that you will not fail.

   Love never fails.

   1 Corinthians 13:8, NASB

3. **Charity is the personal trait that is a good foundation for everything you do.** It is important to be rooted and grounded in love. It is important to have your foundations in love. Whether it is to marry or to serve God, the foundation of love is the best foundation you can have. To be rooted and grounded in love is a better foundation for

what you are doing than to be rooted in hatred, jealousy or greed.

That Christ may dwell in your hearts by faith; that ye, being ROOTED AND GROUNDED IN LOVE, may be able to comprehend with all saints what is the breadth, and length, and depth, and height;

And to know the love of Christ, which passeth knowledge, that ye might be filled with all the fullness of God.

Ephesians 3:17-19

The Old Man's Treasure

A certain man had four sons. His sons used to care for him a lot. They used to visit him and spend time with him often. As he grew older he became less and less wealthy. With time the man's wife died. The widower sought the company of his sons but he did not get it.

His sons were pursuing different dreams and trying to be successful. They also realized that their father was no longer wealthy so they lost interest in him. The old man started feeling so lonely that he sought a way to gain the fellowship of his sons.

One day, after much thought, he approached his friend the carpenter to carve him a beautiful treasure box. He also fixed some gold locks on the box to secure its contents. The old man then filled the box with broken bottles. He placed the box under the dining table. His plan was to deceive his sons that the sound of the bottles was the sound of a great treasure they would inherit from him.

He then invited his sons to a special dinner. During dinner, one of his sons accidentally kicked the box. The sound caught the attention of all the sons and they asked their father about the box. He happily informed them about his treasure that they would inherit at his death. With a treasure to be inherited from their ailing father, the unloving sons were transformed into caring sons. They took turns to spend time with their father and cared for all his needs.

Eventually the old man died and the sons held a great memorial service to honour their father. They invited guests from far and wide and spent a lot of money to honour their father's memory. They were in great expectation for the treasure they would receive after the funeral.

Finally, they sat down together to break open the treasure box which had the golden locks. They almost collapsed when they discovered they had inherited a box of broken bottles of all shapes, colours and sizes.

They looked at each other in disbelief. They had been deceived. After a long deafening silence the oldest brother spoke out. With a trembling voice he said, "We deserve these broken bottles. We were only prepared to love our father when we knew we would get something from him."

Ten Positive Attitudes of "He That Hath"

1. "He that hath" has big visions.

2. "He that hath" focuses on opportunities.

3. "He that hath" is surrounded by helpful people.

4. "He that hath" associates with positive, successful people.

5. "He that hath" is an excellent follower.

6. "He that hath" makes a move in spite of his fear.

7. "He that hath" constantly learns and grows.

8. "He that hath" admires godly people.

9. "He that hath" uses his resources wisely.

10. "He that hath" admires rich and successful people.

Ten Negative Attitudes of "He That Hath Not"

1. "He that hath not" thinks of small things.

2. "He that hath not" focuses on obstacles.

3. "He that hath not" resents rich and successful people.

4. "He that hath not" is surrounded by negative and unhelpful people.

5. "He that hath not" associates with negative or unsuccessful people.

6. "He that hath not" resents godly people.

7. "He that hath not" is stopped by his fears.

8. "He that hath not" thinks he already knows.

9. "He that hath not" will do the jobs that demand the least effort.

10. "He that hath not" is a great waster of opportunities.

Chapter 3

"He That Hath Not" Has Negative Traits That Cause Him to Lose the Little He Has

For IF THESE THINGS BE IN YOU, AND ABOUND, they make *you that YE SHALL* NEITHER *BE* BARREN NOR UNFRUITFUL in the knowledge of our Lord Jesus Christ.

2 Peter 1:8

The Scripture above shows us that if you have certain "things" in you, you will not be unproductive. The "things" that make you productive are *positive traits* like diligence, faith, virtue, temperance etc. In the same way, *negative traits* which contradict positive traits have the effect of making you unproductive and barren. Negative traits are commonly found in the lives of poor and unsuccessful people. Look carefully at the life of "he that hath not" and you will notice an abundance of negative traits. Let us now look at some negative traits and see how they create and perpetuate poverty.

NEGATIVE TRAIT: LYING AND DECEPTION

Lying and Deception defined: Deception is the art of misleading people by false statements or false appearances. The world lives and thrives on deception. Most things are not what you think they are and most people tell lies as second nature. Christians struggle for years to overcome the habits of lying and deceiving. Lying and deception are negative traits that will destroy prosperity. So how exactly do lying and deception make you into "he that hath not"?

Six Things You Must Know about Lying and Deception

1. **Lying and deception are negative traits that bring curses.** A cursed person is a frustrated person. Nothing works out for him and he will always be lamenting about his misfortunes. "Cursed is the deceiver," says the Word of God. The deceiver will be frustrated. The deceiver will not succeed. The deceiver will not be happy. The deceiver will be disappointed.

   But CURSED BE THE DECEIVER, which hath in his flock a male, and voweth, and sacrificeth unto the Lord a corrupt thing: for I am a great King, saith the Lord of hosts, and my name is dreadful among the heathen.

   Malachi 1:14

2. **Lying and deception are coverings for hatred.** When somebody lies to you, the person hates you. The Bible is clear about this and says, "A lying tongue hateth those that are afflicted by it..." (Proverbs 26:28). The Bible also teaches that deception is the covering of someone's hatred for you. "Whose hatred is covered by deceit, his wickedness shall be shown before the whole congregation." (Proverbs 26:26).

A person full of deception and hatred is not going to build anything good. He is an evil person who will self-destruct. The Bible predicts the self-destruction of wicked people. "But the wicked shall be cut off from the earth, and the transgressors shall be rooted out of it" (Proverbs 2:22). "...Men of bloodshed and deceit will not live out half their days..." (Psalm 55:23, NASB).

The Astrologer

Louis XI, the great Spider King of France, had a weakness for astrology. He kept a court astrologer whom he admired, until one day the man predicted that a lady of the court would die within eight days. When the prophecy came true Louis was terrified, thinking that either the man had murdered the woman to prove his accuracy, or that he was so versed in his science that his powers threatened Louis himself. In either case he had to be killed.

One evening Louis summoned the astrologer to his room, high in the castle. Before the man arrived, the king told his servants that when he gave the signal they were to pick the astrologer up, carry him to the window and hurl him to the ground, hundreds of feet below.

The astrologer soon arrived, but before giving the signal, Louis decided to ask him one last question: "You claim to understand astrology and to know the fate of others, so tell me what your fate will be and how long you have to live."

"I shall die just three days before Your Majesty," the astrologer replied.

The king's signal was never given. The man's life was spared. The Spider King not only protected his astrologer for as long as he was alive, he lavished him with gifts and had him tended by the finest doctors. In the end, the astrologer outlived the king by many years.

As you can see from this story, the king and his subjects were lying to each other and deceiving each other. The astrologer and the king actually hated each other and their world thrived on deception. It was a dangerous game of how much each could deceive the other. When you become a Christian you must move away from a life of lying and deception. In the end, lying and deception has a negative effect and you, the liar, are punished for your lying and deception.

3. **Lying and deception are negative traits that cause division and discord among brethren.** "A perverse man spreads strife, and a slanderer separates intimate friends" (Proverbs 16:28, NASB). Such characteristics will never lead to increase. Deception will cause you to lose everything, to divide everything, to fragment everything and to break up everything. Leaders who lie to different sections of their people to please them end up losing everything.

4. **Lying and deception are negative traits of people who imagine evil things.** "Deceit is in the heart of them that imagine evil..." (Proverbs 12:20). A person who

continually imagines evil is not going to become prosperous. The evil that he imagines will be his own downfall. Notice what the Bible says. "Though they intended evil against you and devised a plot they will not succeed ..." (Psalm 21:11, NASB).

The Iron Dealer

A certain businessman once had a great desire to make a long journey. He decided to leave part of his estate with a friend so that if his journey was not successful he would have something to return to. He delivered a great number of bars of iron, which were a principal part of his wealth, in trust to one of his friends. He asked his friend to look after the iron bars for him and he set out on his business trip.

Some time after, having had little success on his business trip, he returned home. The first thing he did was to go to his friend and ask for his iron. But his friend, who owed several sums of money, had sold the iron to pay his own debts. He said to his friend, "Truly friend, I put your iron into a room that was locked and secure, imagining that it would be as secure as a bank. But one day, something terrible happened and a rat which no one could have suspected entered the room and ate up all the iron bars.

"Wow," the businessman said, pretending to believe his friend. "This is a terrible misfortune. I have always known that rats loved eating iron bars and I have suffered terribly from them in the past."

He continued, "Because of my past experience with rats I fully understand what has happened today and how the rat ate up all my iron bars."

When his friend heard this answer, he was extremely pleased that the businessman was so easily taken in by his story of the rat eating the iron. He then decided to invite him to dinner the next day as a consolation for the missing iron. The businessman promised that he would be there.

However, on the way home that day, he met one of his friend's children and he carried him home with him and locked him up in a room.

The next day he went to his friend's house for the dinner. There was chaos in the house and everyone seemed to be in a crisis. He asked, "What's going on here? What is happening?"

"O, my dear friend," answered the other, "I beg you to excuse me, if you do not see me as cheerful as I normally am. I have lost one of my children. I have searched for him in the whole city but I cannot find him."

"O!" replied the businessman, "I am so sad to hear about this tragedy. Indeed, yesterday evening as I departed from here I saw a little chicken flying in the air with a child in its claws. I cannot tell whether it was your child or not."

"What!" Exclaimed the friend, "Are you not ashamed to tell such an egregious lie? How could you have seen a chicken that cannot fly and that weighs one kilo carrying away a boy that weighs forty kilos?"

"Why are you amazed," replied the businessman. "We live in a country where one rat can eat a hundred tons of iron bars. Is it such a wonder for a chicken to fly in such a country? In such a country, is it such a wonder for a little chicken to carry away a weight of forty kilos?"

The friend, upon hearing this realized that the businessman was not such a fool as he had taken him to be. So he begged for forgiveness for cheating the businessman and restored him the value of his iron so he could have his son back.

As you can see from this story, the people in the world thrive on lying and deception, each trying to outwit the other. Lying and deception will not advance your cause. They are negative traits that do not lead to abundance.

5. **Lying and deception are negative traits that cause all your successes to be short-lived.** "The lip of truth shall be established forever: but a lying tongue is but for a moment" (Proverbs 12:19). Because deception is a false foundation what is built on it is short-lived and often comes crumbling down after a while. A marriage built on deception will come crumbling down after a short while. A ministry built on deception will come crumbling down after a short while. This is why deception is such a negative and destructive trait.

6. **Lying and deception are negative traits that lead to punishment and destruction.** "A false witness shall not be unpunished and he that speaketh lies shall perish" (Proverbs 25:18). Punishment and perishing are your future because of your lies and deception. You will become "he that hath not" because of your lies.

NEGATIVE TRAIT: GREED

Greed defined: Greed is the excessive desire to acquire or possess more than one needs or deserves. To be greedy is to be covetous.

Four Things You Must Know about Greed

1. **Greed is a negative trait that will lead to violence in your life.** "And THEY COVET FIELDS, AND TAKE THEM BY VIOLENCE; and houses, and take them away: so they oppress a man and his house, even a man and his heritage" (Micah 2:2).

    Greedy people are so full of a desire for more that they are ready to kill and steal to have it. I have met Christians who are so greedy for money that they looked as though they were ready to kill to have more money.

2. **Greed is a negative personal trait that shortens your life.** Greed will get you into many difficult situations which can shorten your life. Most films depict greedy people struggling to get more money for themselves.

    The prince that wanteth understanding is also a great oppressor: but HE THAT HATETH COVETOUSNESS SHALL PROLONG HIS DAYS.

    Proverbs 28:16

3. **Greed is a negative personal trait that leads to discontentment.**

    Yea, THEY ARE GREEDY dogs which CAN NEVER HAVE ENOUGH, and they are shepherds that cannot understand: they all look to their own way, every one for his gain, from his quarter.

    Come ye, say they, I will fetch wine, and we will fill ourselves with strong drink; and to morrow shall be as this day, and much more abundant.

    Isaiah 56:11-12

4. **Greed is a negative personal trait that can lead to the loss of your life.** Greed can cause you to lose your life. More! More! More! The undisciplined pursuit of more is the cause of the downfall of too many greedy people. Notice how the Scripture warns that greed can take away the life of its owner. In the story below, the greedy old man lost his life because he wanted more even though his life was in danger.

So are the ways of everyone that is GREEDY OF GAIN; WHICH TAKETH AWAY THE LIFE OF THE OWNERS THEREOF.

Proverbs 1:19

The Greedy Old Man

There was an old woodcutter who went to the mountain almost every day to cut wood. It was said that this old man was a miser who hoarded his silver until it changed to gold, and that he cared more for gold than anything else in all the world.

One day a wilderness tiger sprang at him and though he ran he could not escape from it. The tiger carried him off in its mouth. The woodcutter's son saw his father's danger, and ran to save him. He carried a long knife and as he could run faster than the tiger that had a man to carry, he soon overtook them.

His father was not much hurt, for the tiger held him by his clothes. When the old woodcutter saw his son about to stab the tiger he called out in great alarm: "Do not spoil the tiger's skin! Do not spoil the tiger's skin! If you can kill him without cutting holes in his skin we can get many pieces of silver for it. Kill him, but do not cut his body."

While the son was listening to his father's instructions the tiger suddenly dashed off into the forest, carrying the old man where the son could not reach him and he was soon killed.

How sad, for the greedy old man paid with his life for wanting more money. He should have thought of his life and not desired to have more. This is how greed takes away the lives of the owners thereof.

NEGATIVE TRAIT: EVIL SPEAKING

Evil speaking defined: *Evil speaking is all forms of speech that are sinful.* It includes things like criticizing, murmuring, flattering, maligning, backbiting, lying and slandering.

Let all bitterness, and wrath, and anger, and clamour, and EVIL SPEAKING, be put away from you, with all malice (Ephesians 4:31).

Three Things You Should Know about Evil Speaking

1. Evil speaking is a very common negative trait that affects the outcome of your life.

For HE THAT WILL LOVE LIFE, and see good days, LET HIM REFRAIN HIS TONGUE FROM EVIL, and his lips that they speak no guile:

1 Peter 3:10

People do not realize how their lives are destroyed by the negative things that they say. All through the Bible you will see God responding to things that people say. When Miriam criticized Moses, the Bible says, "And the Lord heard it..." (Numbers 12:2). It looks like God listens to our conversations.

Also, when Jesus ministered to the Syro-Phoenician woman, He responded to her very words. She had said to him that she did not mind if He considered her to be a dog. Even the dogs would get the crumbs from the table! Jesus said to her, "...For this saying go thy way, the devil is gone out of thy daughter." She received her healing because of the things she said (Mark 7:29).

Even the things we say in our hearts are noted by the Lord. The woman with the issue of blood who received her healing *said within herself*, "If I may but touch his clothes, I shall be whole" (Mark 5:28). Jesus affirmed that it was her faith that had made her whole. Faith is what you believe in your heart and confess with your mouth.

2. **Evil speaking is a negative personal trait that can shorten your life.** All forms of evil speaking can minister death to you. Lies will kill you. Murmuring will kill you. Murmuring killed all the Jews in the wilderness. Flattery will be exposed for the hypocrisy that it is and the flatterer will be eliminated.

> Death and life are in the power of the tongue: and they that love it shall eat the fruit thereof.
>
> Proverbs 18:21

The Lying Wolf

A very old lion lay ill in his cave. All of the animals came to pay their respects to their king except for the fox. The wolf, sensing an opportunity, accused the fox in front of the lion saying, "The fox has no respect for you or your rule. That is why he hasn't even come to visit you."

Just as the wolf was saying this, the fox arrived, and he overheard these words. Then the lion roared in rage at him but the fox managed to say in his own defense, "And who, of all those who have gathered here has rendered your majesty as much service as I have done: For I have travelled far and wide asking physicians for a remedy for your illness and I have found one."

The lion demanded to know at once what cure he had found and the fox said, "It is necessary for you to flay a wolf alive and then take his skin and wrap it around you while it is still warm." The wolf was ordered to be taken away immediately and flayed alive.

As he was carried off, the fox turned to him with a smile and said, "You should have spoken well of me to his majesty rather than ill."

Indeed, the wolf paid with his life for speaking evil of the fox.

3. **Evil speaking is a product of evil thoughts.** Out of the abundance of the heart the mouth speaks. If you keep thinking evil things you will soon speak them forth. Is there anything good? Is there anything praiseworthy? Is there anything nice? Is there anything lovely? Think on these things. What you think about will eventually come out through your mouth.

...for out of the abundance of the heart the mouth speaketh.

Matthew 12:34

The Praying Old Lady

A man worked in a post office. His job was to process all mail that had illegible addresses. One day a letter came to his desk, addressed in shaky handwriting to God. He thought, "I better open this one and see what it's all about."

So he opened it and it read: "Dear God, I am an 83-year-old widow living on a very small pension. Yesterday someone stole my purse. It had a hundred dollars. In it was all the money I had until my next pension check."

"Next Sunday is Mother's Day, and I had invited my last two friends over for dinner. Without that money, I have nothing to buy food with. I have no family to turn to, and you are my only hope. Can you please help me?"

The postal worker was touched, and went around showing the letter to all the others. Each of them dug into his wallet and came up with a few dollars. By the time he made the rounds, he had collected 96 dollars, which they put into an envelope and sent over to her.

The rest of the day, all the workers felt a warm glow, thinking of the nice thing they had done. Mother's Day came and went, and a few days later came another letter from the old lady to God.

All the workers gathered around while the letter was opened. It read, "Dear God, How can I ever thank you enough for what you did for me? Because of your generosity, I was able to fix a lovely dinner for my friends. We had a very nice day, and I told my friends of your wonderful gift. "By the way, there was 4 dollars missing. It was no doubt those thieving bastards at the post office who took it!"

What a shock!!!! What a sustained shock!!!!!!!! What an aftershock for the workers at the post office!!!! This old lady had bad thoughts about the people at the post office. Her instinct was to see them as thieves and cheats instead of kind-hearted people who bent over to help an old lady. How wrong she was with her evil thoughts.

NEGATIVE TRAIT: IDLENESS

Idleness defined: *Idleness is a state of not working, not being active, not being employed and doing nothing.* Idle people habitually do nothing and avoid work.

Three Things You Should Know about Idleness

1. **Idleness is the negative personal trait that accounts for most of the poverty in the world.**

    Slothfulness casteth into a deep sleep; and an IDLE SOUL SHALL SUFFER HUNGER.

    Proverbs 19:15

2. **Idleness is the negative personal trait that accounts for the decay and deterioration of everything.**

    By much slothfulness the building decayeth; and THROUGH IDLENESS of the hands THE HOUSE DROPPETH THROUGH.

    Ecclesiastes 10:18

3. **Idleness is a negative personal trait that God considers to be a sin.**

    Behold, THIS WAS THE INIQUITY of thy sister Sodom, pride, fulness of bread, and ABUNDANCE OF IDLENESS was in her and in her daughters, neither did she strengthen the hand of the poor and needy.

    Ezekiel 16:49

The Crow and the Rabbit

Mr. Rabbit was walking down the road when he spotted a crow at the tiptop of a very tall tree.

He shouted, "Good Morning, Mr. Crow."

Mr. Crow shouted back down, "Good Morning Mr. Rabbit." Mr. Rabbit shouted up, "Whatcha doin' today?" and the answer shouted back down was, "Absolutely nothin' Mr. Rabbit - Absolutely nothin' and loving it."

Well, that sounded pretty good to Mr. Rabbit, so he shouted back up, "Do you think I could do that too?" Mr. Crow shouted back down, "I don't 'see why not!" So, Mr. Rabbit lay down on the side of the road and began doing "absolutely nothing".

In less than 30 minutes Mr Fox came along and ate up Mr Rabbit for his lunch. Mr Rabbit was shocked that he had been eaten by Mr Fox. But it was a hard lesson for Mr Rabbit. You cannot get away with doing absolutely nothing. You can only get away with doing absolutely nothing if you are at the very top. The crow was at the very top of the tree and that is why he could get away with doing "absolutely nothing."

Very few people, if any, are at the very top and can afford to do absolutely nothing.

NEGATIVE TRAIT: SELFISHNESS

Selfishness defined: Selfishness is the art of thinking about yourself. Jesus Christ came to teach us about breaking out of a life of selfishness. Everyone thinking about only himself has led to a very evil and difficult world. Our world is filled with seven billion selfish and greedy people running around to try and get something for themselves. No wonder we have the chaos that we have.

Selfishness is the root of many evils in our world. Selfishness is the opposite of agape love.

Three Things You Should Know about Selfishness

1. **Selfishness is the negative personal trait at the root of every evil thing in this world.** Jesus Christ came into this world to fight selfishness.

   ...If any man will come after me, let him DENY HIMSELF, and take up his cross, and follow me.

   Matthew 16:24

2. **Selfishness is the negative personal trait that is the root of insincerity and falsehood in the world.**

   Do not eat the bread of a selfish man, or desire his delicacies; for as he thinks within himself, so he is. He says to you, "Eat and drink!" But his heart is not with you. You will vomit up the morsel you have eaten, and waste your compliments.

   Proverbs 23:6 (NASB)

3. **Selfishness is the negative personal trait that makes you think of yourself instead of thinking of others.** Selfishness is the opposite of agape love. Agape love thinks about the other person. What a blessing it is to meet people who are not thinking of themselves but of others!

   Be kindly affectioned one to another with brotherly love; in honour PREFERRING ONE ANOTHER;

   Romans 12:10

The Unselfish Patient

Two men, both seriously ill, occupied the same hospital room. One man was allowed to sit up in his bed for an hour each afternoon to help drain the fluid from his lungs. His bed was next to the room's only window. The other man had to spend all his time flat on his back. The men talked for hours on end. They spoke of their wives and families, their homes, their jobs, their involvement in the military service and where they had been on vacation.

And every afternoon when the man in the bed by the window could sit up, he would pass the time by describing to his roommate all the things he could see outside the window. The man in the other bed began to live for those one-hour periods where his world would be broadened and enlivened by all the activity and colour of the world outside.

The window overlooked a park with a lovely lake. Ducks and swans played on the water while children sailed their model boats. Young lovers walked arm in arm amidst flowers of every colour of the rainbow. Grand old trees graced the landscape, and a fine view of the city skyline could be seen in the distance.

As the man by the window described all this in exquisite detail, the man on the other side of the room would close his eyes and imagine the picturesque scene. One warm afternoon the man by the window described a parade passing by. Although the other man couldn't hear the band - he could see it in his mind's eye as the gentleman by the window portrayed it with descriptive words. Days and weeks passed.

One morning, the day nurse arrived to bring water for their baths only to find the lifeless body of the man by the window, who had died peacefully in his sleep. She was saddened and called the hospital attendants to take the body away. As soon as it seemed appropriate, the other man asked if he could be moved next to the window. The nurse was happy to make the switch, and after making sure he was comfortable, she left him alone.

Slowly, painfully, he propped himself up on one elbow to take his first look at the world outside. Finally, he would have the joy of seeing it for himself. He strained to slowly turn to look out the window beside the bed. To his amazement, it faced a blank wall.

The man could not believe it. He asked the nurse what could have compelled his deceased roommate to describe such wonderful things outside this window. The nurse responded that the man was blind and could not even see the wall.

She said, "Perhaps he just wanted to encourage you."

The patient who died was not thinking about himself but about his fellow patient who equally needed comfort.

NEGATIVE TRAIT: ENVY

Envy defined: *Envy is a feeling of discontent or covetousness with regard to another's advantages, success and possessions.*

Three Things You Must Know about Envy

1. Envy is a negative personal trait that destroys a person from within.

A sound heart is the life of the flesh: but ENVY THE ROTTENNESS OF THE BONES.

Proverbs 14:30

The Scripture calls it rottenness of the bones. Envious people are destroyed from within. They may have everything but are focused on what others have and what others are doing. Envious people are not content. They may look happy on the outside but their hearts are thinking about what others have and what others are doing.

Happiness to an envious person is about what another person has or does not have. They may live in the most beautiful castle, but once the person they fear is smiling in a grass hut somewhere else they are not happy.

A person consumed with envy is not happy because of his diseased soul. The soul of such a person is defective and the person is unwell. I have watched envious people live their lives as though they were on a crusade against their own personal happiness. They do not want to be happy! They only want to focus on the existence of another.

Princess Diana said in her own words that she spent her honeymoon thinking about another woman. She said she thought that every five minutes her husband was secretly calling that woman. Instead of being happy and relishing the moments of glory with her prince, her heart and mind were on another lady. She could think of only one thing – someone else whose existence made her unhappy. Indeed, this is the lot of those who cannot enjoy their own lives without thinking of what the other person may be doing or saying.

Accept your lot and focus on what God has done for you. Your envy is self-destructive and the cruelty of your envy is eating you up.

2. **Envy is a negative personal trait that is as cruel as the grave.**

> ...JEALOUSY IS CRUEL AS THE GRAVE: the coals thereof are the coals of fire, which hath a most vehement flame.
>
> Songs of Solomon 8:6

Anyone who has attended a funeral of a young person cut down in the prime of his life will understand the meaning of the phrase, "as cruel as the grave." Attending the funeral of young fathers, mothers and friends only leaves you with desperate feelings of pain.

It is distressing just to watch grieving families torn apart by death: loved ones are wrenched away from those that depend on them. The meaninglessness of their lives and the hopelessness of their situation cannot be counselled away. A great desolation falls on those left behind and a gnawing and persisting pain consumes them. Can there be anything as cruel as the grave? But the Bible says that jealousy is as cruel as the grave. Jealousy is indeed a very evil thing.

3. **Envy is a negative personal trait whose evil effects are worse than anger and cruelty combined.**

> Wrath is cruel, and anger is outrageous; BUT WHO IS ABLE TO STAND BEFORE ENVY?
>
> Proverbs 27:4

What can be worse than cruelty? Remember that Jesus Christ was crucified because of envy (Mark 15:10). Envy is worse than cruelty because it is a mindless force that drives an individual to eliminate another without mercy or good reason. Envy is a monster that I pray you will not have to contend with.

The Greedy Man and the Envious Man

A greedy man and an envious man met up with a great king who was pleased with them for their good works.

The king said to them, "I desire to reward you for your efforts in the kingdom. One of you may ask something of me and I will give it to him, provided I give twice as much to the other."

The envious person did not want to ask first for he was envious of his companion who would receive twice as much. The greedy man also did not want to ask first since he wanted everything that was to be had. A great argument ensued and the king left the two workers to sort themselves out and decide who would make the request first.

Finally, the greedy man pressed the envious man to be the first to make the request. He threatened him so much that the envious man feared for his life. The greedy man was happy that at last he had won over the envious man and would have twice as much of the reward that was coming to the envious man. The two men got ready to see the king and presented themselves before the throne to make their request.

The envious man spoke as agreed and said, "O great king we are thankful for your generosity and kindness towards us. There is no need for you to do more than you have already done. This shall be our reward and it will suffice us for the rest of our lives."

He continued, "*O great king, please pluck out one of my eyes.* This is something I cannot do for myself and it shall be a sufficient reward for the rest of my life. The greedy person could not believe his ears as he heard the reward that the envious man had chosen. Immediately, he knew that the envious man had done him in.

"I am going to lose both of my eyes," he wailed. "Why was I so greedy? Why did I want twice as much? Why did I trust my life to an envious and cruel man?"

Indeed, he had trifled with the envious man. He never imagined the cruelty that could come out of the envious man. The envious man in his cruelty wanted the two eyes of the greedy man to be taken out to punish him for getting twice as much. The envious man was prepared to lose one eye so that his enemy would be blind. What kind of mindless and senseless wickedness was this? Indeed, you must fear the envious for their cruelty is more than the grave! The greatest sin of men to crucify Jesus Christ was committed because of envy.

For he knew that the chief priests had delivered him for envy.

Mark 15:10

Chapter 4

Research Uncovers the Negative Traits That Cause Poverty and Inequality

Research Reveals the Traits That Lead to Poverty

(Source: Green, Maia (2006), Journal of Development Studies 42 (7): 1108–1129.)

1.   In the United States of America, the most commonly held view of poverty is that people become poor because of personal traits that they have.

2.   It is believed that these traits cause a person to fail in life. The traits that lead to poverty range from personality issues to other traits like laziness and even educational levels.

3.   In America, it is believed that it is always the individual's fault when he fails to climb out of poverty.

4.   Another generally held belief is that poor people are poor because of their own personal failings. Therefore, poor people should not be compensated and assisted by the state.

5.   It is apparent that poor people and poverty are generally viewed in a negative light.

6.   Poverty is therefore viewed as something to be attacked and eradicated. Unfortunately, the negativity towards poverty often leads to an extension of negativity towards poor people themselves.

Research Reveals the Traits That Lead to Intractable Poverty

Source: FAO Corporate Document Repository (Originated by: Economic and Social Development Department.)

1.   Intractable poverty is explained by *a lack of knowledge* and *a lack of good skills* in conjunction with *laziness*. These three things are widely given as the main cause of poverty.

2.   Intractable poverty is most notably caused by *'laziness'* which is characterised by:

a) A low interest in a good life,

b) Passivity,

c) A lack of motivation and initiative,

d) A low intellect,

e) Dependency thinking,

f) Reliance on assistance from others,

g) Lack of life skills to plan and organise their life,

h) Bad training and care of children by parents.

It was felt by some that laziness should be dealt with through education. The overall feeling was that these types of people are 'no hopers' and in need of some form of assistance to survive; they do not have the ability and life skills to manage alone.

3.   The poorest amongst the poor were identified as:

a) Those who were lazy and hopeless

b) Those unable to help themselves

c) Those who lacked interest and skills

d) Those who had large households with many dependent children.

Research Reveals the Traits
That Lead to Inequality

*Source: **Simon Smith Kuznets** (April 30, 1901 – July 8, 1985) was a Russian American economist at the Wharton School of the <u>University of Pennsylvania</u> who won the 1971 <u>Nobel Memorial Prize in Economic Sciences</u> "for his empirically founded interpretation of economic growth which has led to new and deepened insight into the economic and social structure and process of development"*

1. Inter-related, non-linear and complex factors lead to inequality.

There are many reasons for economic inequality within societies.

The causes of inequality are often inter-related, non-linear, and complex.

Acknowledged factors that impact economic inequality include: innate ability, labour, education, race, gender, culture, wealth condensation, development patterns, personal preference for work, leisure and risk.

2. A diversity of personal preferences lead to inequality.

Diversity of preferences within a society often contributes to economic inequality. **When faced with the choice between working harder to earn more money and enjoying more leisure time, equally capable individuals with identical earning potential often choose different strategies**. This leads to economic inequality even in societies with perfect equality in abilities and circumstances.

3. The innate abilities of individuals lead to inequality.

Many people believe that there is a correlation between differences in innate ability, such as intelligence, strength, or charisma, and an individual's wealth.

Such innate abilities might also affect an individual's ability to operate within society in general, regardless of the labour market.

4.   Education levels lead to inequality.

One important factor in the creation of inequality is variation in individuals' access to education. Education, especially in an area where there is a high demand for workers, creates high wages for those with this education.

Chapter 5

"He That Hath" Will Get Even More Because of His Creativity

What You Should Know about Man's Creativity

1. **God created man in His image and therefore man is innately creative.** Man will either use his creativity or not. The world is divided into rich and poor. Most of the poor sections are populated by people who do not use their God-given creativity. Creativity is seen in the innovations, inventions and ideas that men come up with.

    And God said, LET US MAKE MAN IN OUR IMAGE, after our likeness: and let them have dominion over the fish of the sea, and over the fowl of the air, and over the cattle, and over all the earth, and over every creeping thing that creepeth upon the earth.

So GOD CREATED MAN IN HIS *OWN* IMAGE, in the image of God created he him; male and female created he them.

Genesis 1:26-27

2. **God gave man the authority to finish the work of creation.** Man was so creative that God left the finishing of His creation to man. Man was given the awesome job of labelling and naming the created beings.

And out of the ground the LORD God formed every beast of the field, and every fowl of the air; and BROUGHT THEM UNTO ADAM TO SEE WHAT HE WOULD CALL THEM: and whatsoever Adam called every living creature, that was the name thereof.

And Adam gave names to all cattle, and to the fowl of the air, and to every beast of the field; but for Adam there was not found an help meet for him.

Genesis 2:19-20

3. **Men became creators of evil things.** Men misused the creative power God gave them and began to invent evil things.

And even as they did not like to retain God in their knowledge, God gave them over to a reprobate mind, to do those things which are not convenient;

Being filled with all unrighteousness, fornication, wickedness, covetousness, maliciousness; full of envy, murder, debate, deceit, malignity; whisperers,

Backbiters, haters of God, despiteful, proud, boasters, INVENTORS OF EVIL THINGS, disobedient to parents,

Romans 1:28-30

4. **A lack of creativity gives rise to "diminishing returns".**
   The returns you get from farming diminish as the years go
   by. The returns you get from fishing diminish as the years
   go by and the returns you get from mining also diminish
   as the years go by. That is why these activities are called
   "diminishing returns" activities. When people lack
   creativity, they are forced to live off the natural resources
   of their land. This gives rise to farming, fishing and
   mining as the main activities of the people. These
   diminishing returns activities also give rise to hunger,
   poverty, migrations and wars. Diminishing returns is
   recorded in the Bible. In the book of Genesis it is stated
   that the land could not sustain the people.

   For their riches were more than that they might dwell
   together; and the land wherein they were strangers
   could not bear them because of their cattle.

   Genesis 36:7

5. **A lack of creativity causes poverty.** It is a fact that as
   time goes by land yields less and less to its owners. This
   reality is the reason for several patterns that are seen in
   human life and experience.

6. **A lack of creativity gives rise to migrations.** Large
   numbers of people migrating in search of greener pastures
   are evidence of the fact that land yields less and less as the
   years go by. This reality has given rise to the nomadic
   lifestyles of many of the peoples on earth. The Bible has
   clear examples of how diminishing returns from the land
   gave rise to migrations. "For their riches were more than
   that they might dwell together; and the land wherein they
   were strangers could not bear them because of their cattle"
   (Genesis 36:7).

7. **A lack of creativity gives rise to wars.** Wars between nations, tribes and people groups have often been fought over land. They fight because they have no way of prospering without acquiring more land or taking the riches of other people. The need for more land for the purposes of farming, mining, etc., has inspired numerous wars. Hitler invaded Russia because he wanted the resources of Russia to feed his superior German civilization.

Increasing and Decreasing Returns

Creativity always leads to activities that give increasing returns. The terms 'increasing returns' and 'decreasing returns' are used in the world of industry and business. It will be very helpful for you to understand these terms as they throw a lot of light on the causes of poverty and riches. Rich and prosperous countries, people and even churches specialize in 'increasing returns' activities whilst poor countries, poor people and even poor churches specialize in 'decreasing returns' activities. So what are 'increasing returns' activities?

An activity which has 'increasing returns' is often something like running a factory or some kind of industry. An activity which has 'decreasing returns' is often an activity like farming, mining or fishing.

What Are Decreasing Returns?

A lack of creativity gives rise to decreasing returns activities that consist of activities from which the profit gets less and less as the years go by. Usually, decreasing returns are caused by the nature of the work itself. For instance, farming, which is a typical decreasing returns activity, can only yield less and less as the years go by because the land gets worn out and is no more as fruitful as it used to be. Also, there is only a certain amount of investment you can make into a piece of land. Pouring more investments to what you have already put in will not cause the land to give more yield.

If, for instance, you have ten plots of land and you have two tractors that are working the land buying a hundred more tractors will not make the land yield any more produce. In fact, investing like that will make you lose even more money on your already diminishing returns farm. The same thing goes for an activity like mining where the minerals that are being mined are getting finished. More and more investments into the same mine will not make the mine more profitable. Therefore, generally speaking, the owners of the farms and the mines can only expect diminishing profits, less money and less prosperity as the years go by.

What Are Increasing Returns?

On the other hand, 'increasing returns' activities are borne out of creativity and consist of things like manufacturing, running factories, etc., that continue to give higher and higher profits every year (if they are run efficiently). This is because the same initial investment that was made to set up the factory will not need to be made again every year.

For example, if two million dollars was used to set up the factory, the investors may have paid back their bills by the fifth year. This means that from the sixth year onwards they will make more and more profit because they will not have those initial expenses any more. They will continue to make ever-increasing profits from their industry because of this reality.

So whilst the farmer and the miner are experiencing reduced or 'diminishing returns from their farms the operators of the factories and industries will be experiencing increasing and higher profits from their activities.

Creativity is a form of godliness (being like God). This is because God is first and foremost a creator. The unbelievers of this world have used this principle of creativity and it has caused rich countries to get richer. The people who have not used this principle of creativity have caused their poor countries to get even poorer.

Rich and creative countries actually specialize in wealth creating activities (what the economists call 'increasing returns' activities) and poor countries actually specialize in non-creative poverty-causing activities (what the economists call 'decreasing returns' activities).

Rich countries have all become rich in exactly the same way, through policies steering them away from diminishing returns activities and into increasing returns activities like manufacturing.

Rich countries have become superior and dominated poorer countries through creativity. Those who sell iPods and iPads have risen up to dominate those who harvest oranges and groundnuts and tomatoes for a living. Like God, they rule and dominate the world because creativity makes you rise and operate in higher and superior dimensions.

When you hear leaders of third world countries declaring their principal economic goals to be agriculture, you realise that they are actually making their countries specialize in poverty.

What Are Perfect Markets and Imperfect Markets?

Another reason why 'creative increasing returns' activities continue to make people rich is because their products are sold on what is called an 'imperfect market' whereas the products of 'non-creative diminishing returns' activities are sold on 'perfect markets'.

A perfect market is a market in which people cannot change their prices that easily. The price is determined by world forces that are beyond any particular person's control. That means that the farmer does not have any control over the price of the oranges and the pineapples he has worked so hard to produce. In this perfect market he has to read in the newspaper the price of oranges, pineapple and cocoa. And he has to accept it because there is nothing he can do about it. Cocoa, pineapple and oranges are produced in many parts of the world and no one person can decide how much an orange should cost. The perfect world market will decide this for you. I wonder why politicians complain about the low world prices of their country's products. Instead of complaining about the low price of gold, cocoa, bananas, they should lead their countries to specialize in activities which are not dependent on such perfect markets.

An imperfect market on the other hand is where products of increasing returns are sold. The imperfect market is not controlled by anyone. That is why it is imperfect. It is a wild market where everybody does what he wants. Everybody sells his products at the price that he chooses. No one can determine the price of your product for you. No one can tell you that your products are not worth much today.

This means you can ensure that you are not cheated or paid less for your hard work. For instance, Toyota Motor Company produces Land Cruisers and therefore determines the prices of Land Cruisers. A Land Cruiser is made by one company whilst the same oranges are produced by thousands of farmers all over the world.

The manager of the Toyota factory does not have to check in the newspaper how much Land Cruisers are being sold for.

He is the only one in the whole wide world who makes these Land Cruisers.

This year he can sell it for fifty thousand, next year seventy thousand and the next year a hundred thousand dollars.

If you want to buy a Land Cruiser, you simply have to pay the price the he has placed on it. There is no world force that can determine the price of his invention which he called a Land Cruiser.

Farmers and fishermen therefore live in an entirely different world from that of manufacturing businesses. Prices of raw materials fluctuate widely and sometimes unpredictably.

While Silicon Valley establishes the prices of their products, producers of raw materials have to read the newspaper every day to see what the market is willing to pay them.

Innovations and Technological Change

The reason why increasing returns activities lead to much prosperity is because increasing returns activities (factories and manufacturing activities) ride on man's creations which are called innovations and technological changes.

i.   An innovation is a new way of doing old things

ii. An innovation is the introduction of new processes and new methods

iii. An innovation is the introduction of a new invention

iv. An innovation is the provision of something new

v.   An innovation is something improved and better than what exists

vi. An innovation improves the efficiency of an existing process

vii. An innovation usually lowers the cost of doing certain things.

You need to 'innovate and create' in order to manufacture something. It takes much more creativity to manufacture a Mercedes Benz than it does to harvest oranges. The inventors of the iPod and iPhone in California have innovated and created much more than the man harvesting yam and corn on a farm in Africa. Obviously, the incomes of people in California will be higher than the incomes of the people in that African village.

Anytime someone *innovates and creates* he actually walks in the image of God in which he was created.

So God created man in his own image, in the image of God created he him; male and female created he them.

Genesis 1:27

He elevates himself above the life of an ordinary man. Anybody who innovates and creates, lifts himself above the curse and the poverty that afflicts most of the planet earth.

Innovators and creators are paid heavily for their achievements. This is why all nations which have innovated, invented and created things like watches, cars, telephones, televisions, videos, iPods, iPads, computers, aeroplanes, trains, air conditioners, heaters, pianos, guitars, washing machines, cookers, microwave ovens, blenders, motor bikes, etc., have become rich.

This also explains why countries which continue to gather oranges, mangoes, pawpaws and coconuts that have fallen from a tree are poor and will continue to be poor.

They have not innovated or invented anything!

They have specialized in activities of decreasing returns!

They have sold their produce in perfect markets!

They have specialized in poverty!

In many poor countries today the only innovations left for the citizens is to discover clever methods of leaving their own countries and getting into rich countries.

Citizens of poorer countries have thus found diverse creative ways of travelling to rich countries and settling there. They have done this by impersonating others and travelling on other people's passports. Thousands of men have posed as women and many women have posed as men. Unknown to the immigration authorities, men have presented passports that belong to women and been welcomed into the rich countries.

Poor Africans have driven into rich countries in the inside of petrol tankers or by hitching a ride in the engine of huge ships.

Others have walked across the entire Sahara desert or swam across the ocean to get into Europe. Further still, we have seen examples of people hanging onto the under-carriage of huge airliners taking off from Africa only to arrive in Europe as frozen dead bodies.

Pastors must be creative. Businessmen must be creative. Politicians must be creative. You must be creative in your marriage. You must be creative in your work. Creativity will make you become "he that hath". History teaches us that creativity will generate wealth. Even if you do not believe the Bible you will see what history teaches us.

History shows us clearly what will happen in the future. "The thing that hath been, it is that which shall be; and that which is done is that which shall be done: and there is no new thing under the sun" (Ecclesiastes 1:9). Let us now look at the effect of creativity in the history of mankind.

History Shows the Impact of Creativity

1. How Venice and Holland became rich through creative activities

Spain was one of the great seafaring nations of Europe. You will realize that most of South America and Latin America speaks Spanish. This is because they were invaded by the Spaniards who came there in search of gold.

But it became clear to observers in the mid-1500s that the enormous wealth, made up of gold and silver flowing into Spain, through their ships returning from South America, just flowed out again and ended up in two places – Venice and Holland.

Why did this flow of gold and silver finally end up in these two places?

What distinguished Venice and Holland where so much of the Spanish gold ended up?

The answer was simple. Venice and Holland had hardly any agriculture. Both of these places are well known for their swamps and water locked lands. But they had an extensive and diversified industry. The realization spread through Europe that the real gold mines of the world were not the physical gold mines in South America but the manufacturing industry.

Giovanni Botero in his work on what causes the wealth of cities said: *"Such is the power of industry that no mine of silver or gold in New Spain or Peru can compare with it, and the duties from the merchandise of Milan are worth more to the Catholic King than the mines of Potosi and Jalisco."*

Anders Berch (1747), the first economics professor in Sweden, also stated, *"The real gold mines are the manufacturing industries.* Italy is a country in which there is no important gold or silver mine and so is France: yet both countries are rich in money and treasure; thanks to industry."

In various forms, the statement that "manufacturing is the real gold mine" is proven all over Europe.

2. How Spain became poor by specialising in non-creative diminishing returns activities

The discovery of the Americas led to immense quantities of gold and silver flowing into Spain. These huge fortunes were not invested in productive systems but actually led to the de-industrialization of Spain.

In 1558, Spain's Minister of Finance, Luis Ortiz describes the situation in a memorandum to King Philip II: *From the raw materials from Spain and the West Indies – particularly silk, iron and cochinilla (a red dye) which cost them only 1 florin, the foreigners produce finished goods which they sell back to Spain for between 10 and 100 florins.*

Spain is in this way subject to greater humiliations from the rest of Europe than those they themselves impose on the Indians. In exchange for gold and silver the Spaniards offer trinkets of greater or lesser value; but by buying back their own raw materials at an exorbitant price, the Spaniards are made the laughing stock of all Europe.

3.   How Europe decided not to follow the example of non-creative Spain

Spain gradually came to be seen as an example of the type of economic policy a nation should avoid at all costs.

Spain protected her agricultural production, like oil and wine, against foreign competition. But by the end of the sixteenth century, Spain was severely de-industrialized.

It became clear that the riches from the colonies had in fact impoverished rather than enriched Spain's own capacity to produce goods and services.

In contrast, England's Henry VII who came to power in 1485, actively protected and encouraged her industry.

4.   How King Henry VII made England wealthy by ensuring creativity through industrialization

King Henry VII of England, who came to power in 1485 had spent his childhood and youth with an aunt in Burgundy in Europe. There he observed great affluence in an area with woollen textile production. Both the wool and the material used to clean it were imported from England.

When Henry later took over his destitute realm of England, he remembered his adolescence on the Continent. In Burgundy not only the textile producers, but also the bakers and the other craftsmen were well off. England was in the wrong business of farming. The king decided on a policy to make England into a textile-producing nation, and not an exporter of raw materials.

Henry VII created extensive policies to ensure that England would shift from diminishing returns activities to industrial activities.

1. He introduced export duties to discourage the export of raw materials from England. He wanted to force the people of England to manufacture wool instead of just exporting raw materials.

2. He gave tax exemptions to anyone who would manufacture wool from the raw materials.

3. He attracted craftsmen from Holland and Italy who would do manufacturing in England.

A hundred years later Elizabeth I placed an embargo on all raw wool exports from England.

In the eighteenth century Daniel Defoe and other historians saw the wisdom in this strategy which they labelled the 'Tudor Plan' after the kings and queens from that family. Like Venice and Holland, and by the same methods, England prospered from the triple incomes of their industries, raw materials and overseas trade.

5. How creativity, industrialization and increasing returns activities drove malaria out of Europe

Malaria was endemic in Europe for centuries, and the fight against this disease is already documented from the times of the Roman Empire. Historically, malaria was present in areas no one today would associate with the disease: Swiss Alpine valleys as high as 1400 metres above sea level were infested with malaria in the Middle Ages, and the disease had been found as far north as the Kola Peninsula in north-western Russia, beyond the Polar Circle.

Europe got rid of its malaria through industrialization and development.

More advanced and intensive agriculture caused swamps to be drained, and irrigation canals – even hydro-electric power plants – meant that the type of stagnating water where malaria thrived was incompatible with economic development. Huge public health works and eradication systems also freed Europe from malaria.

In the place of this economic development that made Europe rich and malaria-free, Africa gets to keep a colonial economic structure that mainly exports raw materials.

Instead of the development and industrialization that eradicated malaria in Europe, Africa gets free mosquito nets. The core problem that is the foundation of all the poverty is not addressed by these gifts from the west.

6.   How European countries protected their creativity from free trade with the outside world

For several hundred years, Europe's trade policy was based on the principle of maximising the creative industrial sectors of their own country and protecting these creative activities from external competition.

For example, England's economic policy was based on a simple rule: import of raw materials and export of industrial products.

In Europe, they also discovered that countries already wealthy could afford a very different policy from those of countries still poor. In fact, once a country had been solidly industrialized the very same factors that required initial protection now required bigger and more international markets in order to develop and prosper.

European creative industries discovered that once they were successful, the protection that was initially required became counterproductive.

They believed that tariffs were as useful for introducing manufacturing in a country as they are damaging once these are established. This is why free trade (exposing your fledgling creative activities to external competition) must be timed properly.

7. How Mongolia reduced its nation to poverty and backwardness (primitivization) by wiping out 'creative increasing returns activities'

Primitivization is the return to backwardness, poverty and the dark ages by wiping out creative industries and creative manufacturing activities. Under a policy of primitivization, the majority of the people are forced back into non-creative diminishing returns activities. As manufacturing industries die out, many of the poverty-causing non-creative activities take over and dominate the nation.

Before 1991, Mongolia had slowly but successfully built a diversified industrial sector. The share of agriculture in the national product had declined steadily from 60 per cent in 1940 to about 16 percent in the mid-1980s. However, their policies proved exceedingly successful in deindustrializing Mongolia.

Half a century of creative industry-building in Mongolia was virtually annihilated over a period of only four years, from 1991 to 1995. In most industrial sectors, production was down by more than 90 per cent because the country had opened up to the rest of the world in 1991.

By March 2000, the country's previously considerable industrial sector had been virtually eradicated.

Statistics showed that, one by one, all of the country's various industries had disappeared, beginning with the most advanced. Statistics showed that the production of bread was down by 71 percent and the production of books and newspapers by 79 percent. Mongolians, in other words, probably ate and read less than before.

In only a few years, real wages had been almost halved and unemployment was rampant.

The only sectors, according to the national industrial statistics, which were expanding were the production of alcohol which showed minimal growth and the collection and preparation of 'combed down' from birds (to the extent this can be defined as an industry).

Closing down the country's steel mills and newspapers and sending its population out to collect bird down cannot be considered anything but a primitivisation of the economy.

The combination of deindustrialization and deconstruction of the state had created large-scale unemployment in Mongolia. Many people had been forced to return to their ancestral way of living: nomadic pastoralism and herding.

In 1990, before the fall of the Berlin Wall, Mongolians shared their lands with 21 million herding animals – sheep, cows, goats and camels. As a consequence of this, the number of grazing animals had risen from 21 million to 33 million in ten years.

Mongolia opened its economy entirely almost overnight and faithfully followed the advice given by the Washington institutions, the World Bank and the International Monetary Fund to let the market take control. Mongolia was supposed to find its place in the global economy by specializing where its comparative advantage lay.

The result was that the Mongolian economy was driven back from the age of industry to that of pastoralism. The nomadic economy, however, was unable to sustain the population and the industrial system, and the result was an economic catastrophe.

8.   How creativity and innovation generate wealth for the makers of golf balls in America as compared to the makers of baseballs in Honduras and Costa Rica

A comparison of people who work in the same field reveals the advantage of innovation in creating wealth and escaping poverty. As I said earlier, innovation makes a man walk in the image of the Creator and therefore places him above his fellow man who does not walk in creativity.

The world's most efficient producers of baseballs for America's national sport are found in Haiti, Honduras and Costa Rica. Baseballs are still hand-sewn as they were when they were invented. All the engineers and all the capital of the United States have not managed to mechanize baseball production. The wages of the world's most efficient baseball producers are miserable. In Haiti they are around 30 cents an hour. Every baseball is stitched by hand with 108 stitches and each worker is able to sew four baseballs per hour. This is done by hand.

The balls are sold in the USA for about $15 each. Following the political problems in Haiti much of the production was moved to Honduras and Costa Rica. Here the wage level is higher, about $1 per hour.

Golf balls, on the other hand, are a high-tech product. One of its important producers is found in the old whaling town of New Bedford, Massachusetts. Research and development play important roles in production.

Production wages in the New Bedford area amount to between $14 and $16 per hour.

The difference between the wages of a golf ball producer and a baseball producer are because one involves creativity and the other does not. Producing golf balls involves creativity, innovation and technological change. Producing baseballs does not involve creativity, innovation or technological change. Baseball production involves simple stitching by hand.

The market rewards the producer of golf balls with an income of between 12 and 36 times more than the world's most effective producer of baseballs.

9. How creativity and technological change generates wealth for the makers of pyjamas in the United States of America as compared to Guatemala

Creativity gives rise to new technology and innovations that demand new knowledge. People are always paid more for their new knowledge, innovation and technological change.

In the 1980s the following product information could be found on a typical pair of pyjamas sold in the United States: '1. Fabric made in the US, 2. Fabric cut in Guatemala and 3. Pyjamas assembled in Guatemala'.

The fabric production was a mechanized job involving creativity so that aspect of the job was done in the United

States. Cutting and assembling was done in poor countries where they did not have creative technological changes.

One day, new laser technologies were developed which allowed high piles of fabric to be cut automatically and with high precision thus eliminating the need for cheap labour. Since cutting the fabric was now a technology based activity, it was moved to the United States.

Sometime during the 1990s, a new text was found on pyjama labels: 1. 'Fabric produced in the United States, 2. Fabric cut in the United States, 3. Pyjamas assembled in Guatemala'.

As you can see, all high income creative jobs are moved to rich countries. Poor countries are left with jobs that do not require creativity.

10. How wealth was increased by creativity, skill and knowledge on the western side of Cuba that grew tobacco, as compared to the other side which grew sugarcane

From an economic point of view, Cuba had an absolute advantage in two tropical crops: sugar and tobacco. Tobacco was predominantly grown on the western part of the island and created a middle class. Sugar – grown on the rest of the island – created two classes of people: masters and slaves.

The cultivation and picking of tobacco created a demand for two specialized skills: tobacco leaves are harvested individually and the market price of the product depended on the creativity and skill of the picker.

Growing tobacco bred skills, creativity, individuality and modest wealth. Where tobacco required skills, care and judgment, sugar only required brute force in cutting the commodity.

A skilled tobacco selector can distinguish seventy or eighty different shades of tobacco; whereas for the cutting of cane, timing is not important.

Tobacco is delicately cut lead by leaf with a small sharp knife, making sure that the rest of the plant survives. However, the sugar plant is simply brutally slashed with a big machete. Working with sugar is a trade; working with tobacco an art.

The origins of the wealth of western Cuba and the poverty of the eastern part of the island are clear: the wealth and prosperity of the west are related to doing a more creative job.

11. How New Zealand became rich by refusing anything that would prevent their country from developing in creativity and industrialization

A book called "A New Zealand Colonist" reveals the mindset of settlers in New Zealand in 1897:

1. The New Zealand settler refuses to accept cheap imports, because accepting them would prevent his country from becoming industrialized.

2. The New Zealand settler discards all theories of free trade with the outer world and levies high import duties on every product, which his colony is capable of supplying. The New Zealanders believe that only in this way can their new land be made a prosperous field.

3. The New Zealander believes that prosperity would not be attainable while subject to unrestricted competition from outsiders. They refused to have the surplus stocks which others dumped on their markets.

4. The New Zealander colonist desires that children growing up around him should have opportunities of *acquiring mechanical skill, and so be saved from becoming mere hewers of wood and drawers of water for richer nations.* He regards mechanical skill and the great products of that skill as the buttress of a people's strength and safety.

5. The New Zealand colonist does not regard immediate results. His eye is on the future and on the children growing up around him.   This settler recently established country, New Zealand, sums up centuries of wisdom.

Is it not ironical that today we find rich countries dumping their surplus products in the poor countries, which see this as a bonus?

In the hierarchy of nations a country that did not protect its industry would have all its creativity doomed to the biblical curse of being branded as 'hewers of wood and drawers of water' (Joshua 9:23). This phrase was commonly used also in the United States as part of the string of argument for protecting manufacturing industries.

The Bible thus recognizes a hierarchy of skills where hewers of wood and drawers of water are located at the bottom.

The Advantages of Creativity

1.   Creativity will change your life completely.

Creativity helps you to change the old things in your life by introducing new methods, ideas, or products. You will benefit from the privileges and outcomes of your ideas. This will make you competitive and you will learn how to win at all costs. You will learn the need to achieve in everything you do. You will learn the need to be first and not second or third.

Creativity will make you a hard worker. You must be creative because it will make you a hard worker and a strong leader who has his own goals. Creativity will boost your confidence as you achieve greater and greater results.

Creativity will cause you to develop in practical wisdom and common sense. You must be creative because you will learn a lot of common sense and good judgment.

2. Creativity will make you into a truly successful person.

You must be creative because it will make you successful in spite of your age, sex or educational level. "During the1950s, 60s and 70s the large majority of people starting companies were in their 30s and 40s. Not true during the 1980s or today, Steve Jobs and Steve Wozniak were both in their early 20s when they started Apple Computers Inc. At the other extreme Ray Kroc was 59 when he started the McDonalds' restaurant chain."

Until recently, entrepreneurship was considered by many to be an all male affair. This is no longer true as more businesses are now being started by women than are being started by men.

Knowledge and skill are very important. However, how you acquire your skills and knowledge is less important. In some cases, university degrees have been known to be a handicap rather than an asset. One researcher suggested recently that one of the biggest handicaps you can have when you start a business is a PhD. For example, Bill Gates, founder of Microsoft left Harvard after his second year.

3. Creativity will make you enjoy your work.

Most people who work in regular jobs get exhausted at the end of the day and dread the morning of the next day, especially after weekends. Now, an entrepreneur works all the time and thus puts all of his energy into his work. By working this hard, he enjoys whatever he does and because of this, whatever venture he puts his effort into, will eventually turn out to be a great success.

Work is often what one is forced to do. Creative people do things because they love doing them. Creative people do not work primarily to enjoy the pleasures of the rich. Getting to execute his ideas is what satisfies him. For a true entrepreneur, work is not a means to an end. It is an end in itself. The process is as rewarding to him as is the end product. Because an entrepreneur is consumed by his desire to work hard, he gets really no time to engage in trivialities of everyday life.

4. Creativity will allow you to be in control of your life.

The best thing about a creative person is that he creates his own life and is in absolute control of his life. He does not have to report to anybody. He can take a vacation any time he feels he needs one. He gets to decide what can happen in his venture. Best of all, nobody can fire him. It is great to be your own boss and to create your own destiny.

5. Creativity will allow you to experience real success.

Very few get to experience real success. Creative people accept the challenges, work hard to overcome them and when victory results, they savour the moment. Even when they fail in the beginning, they do not give up.

Chapter 6

"He That Hath" Will Get Even More Because of His Ability to Recognize the People God Has Sent into His Life

Recognize God's Provision through People

...you did not recognize the time of your visitation.

Luke 19:44 (NASB)

Indeed, God visits His people to bless them and prosper them. It is important to recognize when God visits you to provide for you. Do not think that God provides for only some of His children. You wouldn't do that to your children! So why would you think that God Almighty would care for some of His children and leave others destitute? That is not the case. The problem is that we often cannot recognize

93

God's provision to us because we know of only one way in which He visits us.

The disciples walked several miles with the Lord but did not recognize Him. Isn't that amazing? "After that he appeared in another form unto two of them, as they walked, and went into the country" (Mark 16:12).

The Lord told Adam and Eve to look around them and see that He had provided everything that they needed.

Perhaps if they had not looked around they would not have noticed that everything they needed was already there. You need to become a master at discerning how God has provided for you.

When people do not recognize His provision for what it is, they ignore it and start complaining. The problem is that we often want God to do things in a particular way. Like Naaman the Syrian who expected the prophet to minister the healing in a particular way, we often expect God to meet our needs in a particular way.

I may not live or work in America but in different ways I see how God has provided for me too. Many doctors in America cannot have servants, drivers, security guards or secretaries attending to them. But in the third world I can afford these things. I see them as a provision of God that completely changes the quality of my life.

Understand how God provides so that you do not drive away people God has sent to you.

You must go further and develop the provisions that God has made for you. No matter what provision you have it is your duty to develop it and use it.

Saul was anointed by the Lord but not everybody believed in him. As the Scripture below shows, some even asked,

"How can this man help us?" But others believed in Saul because God had touched their hearts.

And Saul also went home to Gibeah; and there went with him a band of men, whose hearts God had touched. But the children of Belial said, HOW SHALL THIS MAN SAVE US? And they despised him, and brought him no presents. But he held his peace.

1 Samuel 10:26-27

God will touch the hearts of some people and they will love you and serve you.

But God does not touch the hearts of everyone. You must accept and receive the people whom God is touching and sending. They are the greatest blessings and assets in your life.

You will accomplish great things when you recognize the people God has sent into your life. When I look around I see wonderful people whom God has touched and sent into my life. Through these people I have soared higher and higher and achieved more for the Lord.

1.   *"HE THAT HATH" RECOGNIZES BLESSED PEOPLE WHO HAVE BEEN SENT INTO HIS LIFE.*

And Laban said unto him, I pray thee, if I have found favour in thine eyes, *tarry*: for I have learned by experience that THE LORD HATH BLESSED ME FOR THY SAKE.

Genesis 30:27

God may choose *to provide for you* through your association with a blessed person. Laban, the uncle of Jacob, recognized that he had become prosperous because of the presence of Jacob. He recognized it and he said it plainly.

Indeed, you may not come into wealth through your job, your education, your skills or degrees but rather through your *association* with someone. This is one of the greatest principles of prosperity. God often gives one person a very large gift and expects a lot of people to benefit from that gift. God gives wealth to one person and expects a lot of others to enjoy themselves in the shadow of that wealth.

God does not give visions and dreams to everyone. He gives great visions and dreams to one person and expects the others to live under its effect.

Mary Magdalene is the one who was privileged to have a life-like vision of Jesus at the tomb. Even Peter, James and John did not have that vision. You and I did not have that vision and yet we all benefit from it.

God does not give everybody the same gift. Be humble and associate with blessed people so that you may at least receive a few drops of blessing into your life.

2. "HE THAT HATH" RECOGNIZES POOR PEOPLE WHOM GOD HAS SENT INTO HIS LIFE.

Many of us rule out poor people as a source of financial blessing. We assume that prosperity and financial help will only come from the rich, wealthy and famous. However, God sometimes uses poor people to prosper others. Elijah was to be sustained by a starving widow. God used a starving widow to keep Elijah alive during the famine.

Arise, get thee to Zarephath, which belongeth to Zidon, and dwell there: behold, I have commanded

a widow woman there to sustain thee.

1 Kings 17:9

Banks are made rich by the little contributions of many poor people. Insurance companies are propped up by the meagre subscriptions of the masses. Many pastors are sustained by the contributions of their numerous, but poor members. Many politicians win elections because of the votes of the poor people.

These examples show you that people can and do become prosperous through the help of poor people. Also, a poor man can become rich overnight.

Perhaps, this is why the Scripture teaches us to give respect to all men.

...to speak evil of no one, to be peaceable, gentle, SHOWING ALL HUMILITY TO ALL MEN.

Titus 3:2-3, NKJV

3. *"HE THAT HATH" RECOGNIZES MEN OF GOD WHO HAVE BEEN SENT INTO HIS LIFE.*

Failing to recognize the contribution a man of God has made to your life is the ungratefulness that attracts many a curse. Notice the contribution of Elisha to this woman's life.

Now there cried a certain woman of the wives of the sons of the prophets unto Elisha, saying, Thy servant my husband is dead; and thou knowest that thy servant did fear the Lord: and the creditor is come to take unto him my two sons to be bondmen.

And Elisha said unto her, What shall I do for thee? tell me, what hast thou in the house? And she said,

Thine handmaid hath not any thing in the house, save a pot of oil.

Then he said, Go, borrow thee vessels abroad of all thy neighbours, even empty vessels; borrow not a few.

And when thou art come in, thou shalt shut the door upon thee and upon thy sons, and shalt pour out into all those vessels, and thou shalt set aside that which is full.

So she went from him, and shut the door upon her and upon her sons, who brought the vessels to her; and she poured out.

And it came to pass, when the vessels were full, that she said unto her son, Bring me yet a vessel. And he said unto her, there is not a vessel more. And the oil stayed.

Then she came and told the man of God. And he said, Go, sell the oil, and pay thy debt, and live thou and thy children of the rest.

2 Kings 4:1-7

Elisha was an agent of prosperity to the widow. Through his ministry, her oil was multiplied, her bills were paid, her sons were delivered from slavery and her life was changed forever.

One day, I was in Tulsa, Oklahoma, attending a Kenneth Hagin conference. In the middle of the conference, the Spirit of the Lord told me to honour Kenneth Hagin with an offering. But that night, Kenneth Hagin himself described how prosperous he was and how much money he had paid as tithes that year.

I thought to myself, "This man will not need my measly offering."

That night, the Lord dealt with me and showed me how important it was to honour him no matter how small the offering was. The Lord showed me how I had benefited from Kenneth Hagin's ministry. But there was one thing that surprised me. God showed me how every car I had, the house that I lived in and the money I had, had come through Kenneth Hagin's ministry. He showed me that even the ability to travel to Tulsa, had somehow come to me through the ministry of Kenneth Hagin.

As I thought through my life I realised how true it was. God had anointed me through his ministry and everything I had, had come to me because of the anointing I received.

You see, a prophet is an agent of change! A prophet is an agent of prosperity! A prophet is an agent of promotion! And God had sent a prophet into my life. It was imperative that I honoured him because not to honour him was the same as not saying thank you.

4.   *"HE THAT HATH" RECOGNIZES FATHERS THAT HAVE BEEN SENT INTO HIS LIFE.*

Wealth runs in earthly families! The anointing runs in spiritual families! It is important to recognize the fathers that God has sent into your life. If you fail to recognize these fathers you will never join the right family. The wealth and the anointing that is intended for your family will then be lost.

Wealth is passed down from generation to generation. It is important to recognize that the greatest indirect gift of prosperity that may come to you from your father is an education. Even the suggestion to go to school and the advice of what to study in school are sources of prosperity.

Not all fathers have the ability to leave their children direct wealth and property. However, in some cases, God does put wealth directly in your hand through your father. Be open to receive prosperity through your father. Notice how Abraham's wealth came into the hands of Isaac.

> And Abraham gave all that he had unto Isaac. But unto the sons of the concubines, which Abraham had, Abraham gave gifts, and sent them away from Isaac his son, while he yet lived, eastward, unto the east country.
>
> Genesis 25:5-6

5. "HE THAT HATH" RECOGNIZES FRIENDS OF HIS FATHER WHO HAVE BEEN SENT INTO HIS LIFE.

Even the friends of your father can be a source of wealth. That is why you must not remove the ancient landmarks. That is why you must not break important family relationships. If you despise your father and his friendships, you may cut yourself off from potential sources of wealth. Solomon wisely related with his father's friends. King David, Solomon's father had a good friend called Hiram. Solomon maintained a good relationship with Hiram and benefited greatly from his father's friend.

> And Hiram king of Tyre sent his servants unto Solomon; for he had heard that they had anointed him king in the room of his father: *for Hiram was ever a lover of David...*
>
> And it came to pass, when Hiram heard the words of Solomon, that he rejoiced greatly, and said, Blessed be the Lord this day, which hath given unto David a wise son over this great people. And Hiram sent to Solomon, saying, I have considered the things which thou sentest

to me for: and I will do all thy desire concerning timber
of cedar, and concerning timber of fir.

...So Hiram gave Solomon cedar trees and fir trees
according to all his desire.

1 Kings 5:1, 7-8,10

6. *"HE THAT HATH" RECOGNIZES THE IMPORTANCE OF THE MARRIAGE PARTNER GOD HAS SENT TO HIM.*

And *Naomi had a kinsman of her husband's, a mighty
man of wealth*, of the family of Elimelech; and his name
was Boaz. And Ruth the Moabitess said unto Naomi,
Let me now go to the field, and glean ears of corn after
him in whose sight I shall find grace. And she said unto
her, Go, my daughter. And she went, and came, and
gleaned in the field after the reapers: and her hap was to
light on a part of the field belonging unto Boaz, who
was of the kindred of Elimelech.

Ruth 2:1-3

Some people are blessed and prosper by marrying into a
prosperous family. Do not be ashamed if that is the way God
chooses to lift you up. There are many beautiful ladies who
have been lifted into important places through their marriage
to a particular person. There are also men who have prospered
by marrying into rich families.

Unfortunately, there are always people who do not want to
accept this fact. It punctures their ego to accept that their lives
have been changed because of who they married. They wish
they could say, "I would have prospered anyway if I hadn't
married you." This attitude leads to ingratitude. Such people
are presumptuous and ungrateful. It is important to recognize

that there are many replacements waiting in the shadows to take over from presumptuous and ungrateful spouses who never acknowledge the blessing that has come upon them through their partners.

Sometimes, God chooses a humbling method to prosper you. If you are not humble you will not be able to enter into nor enjoy the blessing.

7. *"HE THAT HATH" RECOGNIZES THE IMPORTANCE OF THE BROTHERS GOD HAS GIVEN TO HIM.*

God can bless you through your brother, even your little brother. You may want it to be some other way but God could choose to use your own brothers. Even more humbling could be the fact that God would use your brother whom you despised, ridiculed, teased and rejected. This is what happened to Joseph's brothers. They had to accept the provision of God from the brother they had despised. Humble yourself and become someone who can receive God's provision through your own brother.

> And Joseph placed his father and his brethren, and gave them a possession in the land of Egypt, in the best of the land, in the land of Rameses, as Pharaoh had commanded.
>
> And Joseph nourished his father, and his brethren, and allhis father's household, with bread, according to their families.
>
> And there was no bread in all the land; for the famine was very sore, so that the land of Egypt and all the land of Canaan fainted by reason of the famine.
>
> Genesis 47:11-13

8. "HE THAT HATH" RECOGNIZES THE IMPORTANCE OF THE STRANGERS GOD SENDS TO HIM.

Great blessings came to the family of Zipporah when they received a stranger called Moses into their lives.

We are often wary of strangers and only expect blessings to come through people we know. But God can use an absolute stranger to bring you into prosperity. The Scripture encourages us to entertain strangers because sometimes a stranger is an angel in disguise. That is why you must be open and polite to all and sundry.

...But Moses fled from the face of Pharaoh, and dwelt in the land of Midian: and he sat down by a well.

Now the priest of Midian had seven daughters: and they came and drew water, and filled the troughs to water their father's flock.

And the shepherds came and drove them away: but Moses stood up and helped them, and watered their flock.

And when they came to Reuel their father, he said, How is it that ye are come so soon to day?

And they said, An Egyptian delivered us out of the hand of the shepherds, and also drew water enough for us, and watered the flock.

And he said unto his daughters, And where is he? why is it that ye have left the man? call him, that he may eat bread.

And Moses was content to dwell with the man: and he gave Moses Zipporah his daughter.

Exodus 2:15-21

9. "HE THAT HATH" RECOGNIZES THE IMPORTANCE OF THE ENEMIES GOD HAS ALLOWED INTO HIS LIFE.

Many people tremble when they encounter enemies in their lives and ministry. Ironically, these enemies are often used by the Lord to bring greatness into your life. You must trust the Lord and learn to say, "God is great!" You must learn to recognize that sometimes God does use your enemy to make you advance to your destiny. It is not only your friends who can help you. You can be helped by an enemy. In fact, the enemy often brings out the best in you. Your enemy will do for you what your friend cannot do. See the enemy in a different light.

Watch for how their stubbornness, their wickedness, their treachery, their envy and hatred are being used by the Lord to enhance your life!

All things work together for good and God can and will bless you through your enemies. Not only will you overcome your enemies but these enemies will be used to make you into a greater person.

Ten Examples of Help Coming through the Enemy

1) **Jesus was helped by the treachery and disloyalty of Judas.** Jesus Christ's greatest achievement was the saving of the world through His death on the cross. Our Lord Jesus was helped to the cross by the betrayal of Judas.

Then Judas, which had betrayed him ... Saying, I have sinned in that *I have betrayed the innocent blood.* And they said, what is that to us? See thou to that.

Matthew 27:3-4

2) **Jesus was helped to the cross by the jealousy of the Pharisees.** The Scripture tells us that Jesus was delivered because of the envy of the Pharisees.

But Pilate answered them, saying, Will ye that I release unto you the King of the Jews?

For he knew that the chief priests had delivered him for envy.

Mark 15:9-10

3) **Moses was helped by the stubbornness of Pharaoh.** Moses' greatest accomplishment was the deliverance of Israel through fantastic signs and wonders that he performed. Pharaoh gave Moses the opportunity to perform more wonders by stubbornly refusing to let the people go.

And there arose not a prophet since in Israel like unto Moses, whom the Lord knew face to face,

In all the signs and the wonders, which the Lord sent him to do in the land of Egypt to Pharaoh, and to all his servants, and to all his land, and in all that mighty hand, and in all the great terror which Moses shewed in the sight of all Israel.

Deuteronomy 34:10-12

4) **Joseph was helped by the wickedness of his brothers.** Joseph's ministry as a Prime Minister of Egypt came

about because Joseph's brothers helped to transfer him to the country in which he would be the Prime Minister. They inadvertently transferred him to the land of his exaltation and promotion.

And Judah said unto his brethren, What profit is it if we slay our brother, and conceal his blood?

Come, and let us sell him to the Ishmeelites, and let not our hand be upon him; for he is our brother and our flesh. And his brethren were content....

And the Midianites sold him into Egypt unto Potiphar, an officer of Pharaoh's, and captain of the guard.

Genesis 37:26-27, 36

5) **Paul was helped by the wickedness of the Jews.** Paul's greatest achievements were his letters that still speak to the worldwide church. It was when Paul was in prison that he was able to write these letters to the church. Notice how he wrote his letters from prison.

PAUL, A PRISONER of Jesus Christ, and Timothy our brother, unto Philemon our dearly beloved, and fellowlabourer,

And to our beloved Apphia, and Archippus our fellowsoldier, and TO THE CHURCH IN THY HOUSE:

Philemon 1:1-2

6) **Paul was helped by the buffeting of the messenger of Satan.** Through this messenger, who was allowed to buffet him, he was kept from the sin of pride. Through this messenger of Satan, Paul's infirmities were magnified and the power of Christ rested on his life. Paul became

more powerful, more anointed just because of the enemy who was let loose on his life.

And lest I should be exalted above measure through the abundance of the revelations, there was given to me a thorn in the flesh, THE MESSENGER OF SATAN to buffet me, lest I should be exalted above measure.

For this thing I besought the Lord thrice, that it might depart from me.

And he said unto me, My grace is sufficient for thee: for my strength is made perfect in weakness. Most gladly therefore will I rather glory in my infirmities, THAT THE POWER OF CHRIST MAY REST UPON ME.

2 Corinthians 12:7-9

7) **David was helped by the backslidden and demon-possessed King Saul to become an anointed psalmist.** The Psalms of David are his greatest legacy to us. After thousands of years, the anointed Psalmist ministers to us out of the troubles he encountered from the trials and persecution of King Saul.

8) **Daniel was helped by the accusations of the princes and presidents of Dairus' kingdom.** Daniel prospered and had even greater favour after he came out of the lions' den alive. Daniel's God was respected and accepted as the one true God after he survived the experience in the lions' den. God used the jealousy, hatred and undermining of his colleagues to bring Daniel to the highest possible position.

Then king Darius wrote unto all people, nations, and languages, that dwell in all the earth; Peace be multiplied unto you.

I make a decree, That in every dominion of my kingdom men tremble and fear before the God of Daniel: for he is the living God, and stedfast for ever, and his kingdom that which shall not be destroyed, and his dominion shall be even unto the end.

He delivereth and rescueth, and he worketh signs and wonders in heaven and in earth, who hath delivered Daniel from the power of the lions.

So this Daniel prospered in the reign of Darius, and in the reign of Cyrus the Persian.

Daniel 6:25-28

9) **Job was helped by the destructive attacks of Satan to become twice as rich as he originally was.** Through the attacks of Satan things worked out which ensured that Job would climb to the pinnacle of material prosperity.

And the Lord turned the captivity of Job, when he prayed for his friends: also the Lord gave Job twice as much as he had before.

Job 42:10

10) **Ruth was helped by the death of her husband and her sons.** Death is the last and greatest enemy of mankind. Through death Ruth was forced to go back to Bethlehem. It was there that she became the great grandmother of David and joined the genealogy of Jesus Christ.

And Salmon begat Booz of Rachab; and Booz begat Obed of Ruth; and Obed begat Jesse; And Jesse begat David the king; and David the king begat Solomon of her *that had been the wife* of Urias;

Matthew 1:5-6

Chapter 7

"He That Hath" Will Get Even More Because He Recognizes the Place of His Blessing

And Jacob awaked out of his sleep, and he said, SURELY THE LORD IS IN THIS PLACE; and I knew *it* not.

Genesis 28:16

Good things that are determined for your life are connected to certain locations. Throughout the Bible, you will find God asking people to travel away from certain places or to stay in certain places. Apparently, blessings do not happen everywhere! Physical locations are significant in determining whether you will experience certain blessings or not. When a tree is planted in the wrong place it does not flourish. The Bible teaches us that we are trees of righteousness, the planting of the Lord. We have been planted in particular places for particular reasons.

Jacob recognized that the Lord was in the place where he had slept. So he said, "The Lord was in this place, and I knew it not." You must be able to recognize where God is, as far as you are concerned. You must stay where God is.

Isaac moved from place to place until he found somewhere that God had made a room for him. He called that place Rehoboth. He knew that he would be fruitful because he had finally found the place that God wanted him to be planted.

> And he removed from thence, and digged another well; and for that they strove not: and he called the name of it Rehoboth; and he said, for now the Lord hath made room for us, and we shall be fruitful in the land.
>
> Genesis 26:22

When you find the place that God has designed for you, you will become fruitful. This is the reason why I transfer pastors from place to place. I am searching for their Rehoboth, where they will become fruitful and flourish in the ministry. This is the reason why I have stayed in certain places, because I have sensed that God had determined to prosper me in those places.

1. "HE THAT HATH" WILL GET MORE BECAUSE HE RECOGNIZES WHEN GOD HAS CHOSEN TO PROSPER HIM OUT OF HIS HOME COUNTRY.

Several people received their gifts of prosperity when they travelled out of their home country. There is a truth that a prophet is not accepted in his own country. I used to feel that the whole Bible was true except that verse. My reason was simple. When I held a healing service in my church I experienced miracles, signs and wonders. I felt no lack of honour in my own home or church. But one day, the Lord arranged another crusade for me in a far away country. There, I saw blind eyes opened, the cripples walking and even the dead raised. Then I realised that God had honoured me with far greater miracles than when I was in my own church.

Seven People Who Prospered Because They Travelled Away from Their Home Country

a. Abraham prospered when he travelled away from his home country.

And Abram went up out of Egypt, he, and his wife, and all that he had, and Lot with him, into the south.

And Abram was very rich in cattle, in silver, and in gold.

Genesis 13:1-2

b. Jacob prospered when he travelled to live with his uncle Laban.

I am not worthy of the least of all the mercies, and of all the truth, which thou hast shewed unto thy servant; for with my staff I passed over this Jordan; and now I am become two bands.

Genesis 32:9-10

c. Joseph became the Prime Minister when he travelled to Egypt, albeit under very difficult circumstances.

And Judah said unto his brethren, What profit is it if we slay our brother, and conceal his blood?

Come, and let us sell him to the Ishmeelites, and let not our hand be upon him; for he is our brother and our flesh. And his brethren were content.

Then there passed by Midianites merchantmen; and they drew and lifted up Joseph out of the pit, and sold Joseph to the Ishmeelites for twenty pieces of silver: and THEY BROUGHT JOSEPH INTO EGYPT.

Genesis 37:26-28

And PHARAOH SAID UNTO JOSEPH, See, I HAVE SET THEE OVER ALL THE LAND OF EGYPT.

And Pharaoh took off his ring from his hand, and put it upon Joseph's hand, and arrayed him in vestures of fine linen, and put a gold chain about his neck;

And he made him to ride in the second chariot which he had; and they cried before him, Bow the knee: and he made him ruler over all the land of Egypt.

Genesis 41:41-43

d. Lot became prosperous when he travelled with Abraham on his journey into the Promised Land.

And Abram was very rich in cattle, in silver, and in gold.

And he went on his journeys from the south even to Bethel, unto the place where his tent had been at the beginning, between Bethel and Hai;

Unto the place of the altar, which he had made there at the first: and there Abram called on the name of the Lord.

AND LOT ALSO, WHICH WENT WITH ABRAM, HAD FLOCKS, AND HERDS, AND TENTS.

Genesis 13:2-5

e. Ruth travelled from Moab to Bethlehem and became the prosperous wife of Boaz and great grandmother of King David.

And Ruth said, Intreat me not to leave thee, or to return from following after thee: for whither thou goest, I will go; and where thou lodgest, I will lodge: thy people shall be my people, and thy God my God:

Where thou diest, will I die, and there will I be buried: the Lord do so to me, and more also, if ought but death part thee and me.

When she saw that she was stedfastly minded to go with her, then she left speaking unto her.

SO THEY TWO WENT UNTIL THEY CAME TO BETHLEHEM...

Ruth 1:16-19

And Salmon begat Booz of Rachab; and BOOZ BEGAT OBED OF RUTH; and Obed begat Jesse;

And JESSE BEGAT DAVID THE KING; and David the king begat Solomon of her that had been the wife of Urias;

Matthew 1:5-6

f. Paul became the first and great missionary because he travelled so far away from his home.

As they ministered to the Lord, and fasted, the Holy Ghost said, Separate me Barnabas and Saul for the work whereunto I have called them.

And when they had fasted and prayed, and laid their hands on them, they sent them away.

So they, being sent forth by the Holy Ghost, departed unto Seleucia; and from thence THEY SAILED TO CYPRUS.

And when they were at SALAMIS, they preached the word of God in the synagogues of the Jews: and they had also John to their minister.

Acts 13:2-5

g. Jesus became a miracle-working healing Jesus when He travelled away from Bethlehem to Galilee. Jesus was not able to do the same level of miracles in his home country.

And he could THERE do no mighty work, save that he laid his hands upon a few sick folk, and healed them.

Mark 6:5

...Ye will surely say unto me this proverb, Physician, heal thyself: whatsoever we have heard done in Capernaum, DO ALSO HERE IN THY COUNTRY.

And he said, Verily I say unto you, No prophet is accepted in his own country.

Luke 4:23-24

2. "HE THAT HATH" RECOGNIZES THE IMPORTANCE OF STAYING IN HIS HOME COUNTRY.

It is also equally possible to prosper by staying in your own country. Just as people have prospered by travelling away from home, many others have prospered by staying. It all depends on what the Holy Spirit wants you to do.

There is no fixed formula in God's plan for you. It may be better for you to go or it may be better for you to stay. Some people prosper when they travel and others prosper when they stay home. Isaac prospered when he stayed because God had told him to stay put instead of travelling away from the famine-struck region. But in many other cases, like Abraham, it was the will of God for them to leave home.

And there was a famine in the land, beside the first famine that was in the days of Abraham. And Isaac went unto Abimelech king of the Philistines unto Gerar. And the LORD appeared unto him, and said, GO NOT DOWN INTO EGYPT; DWELL IN THE LAND which I shall tell thee of:

Genesis 26:1-2

Chapter 8

"He That Hath" Will Get Even More Because He Recognizes the Grace of God

For the grace of God that bringeth salvation hath appeared to all men,

Titus 2:11

It is important to recognize the grace of God when it is working. People do not recognize the grace of God and do not take advantage of it. God will bless you and do things in your life that are the grace of God in action. Failing to recognize this grace will cause you to ignore it, refuse it or even reject it. Paul spoke about how the apostles had recognized the grace of God that was on his life for the evangelism of the Gentiles.

...and RECOGNIZING THE GRACE THAT HAD BEEN GIVEN TO ME, James and Cephas and John, who were reputed to be pillars, gave to me and Barnabas the right hand of fellowship, so that we *might go* to the Gentiles, and they to the circumcised.

***They* only *asked* us to remember the poor--the very thing I also was eager to do.**

Galatians 2:9-10 (NASB)

When you recognize the grace of God, you will make the most of it and develop under it. Paul wrote to Timothy and asked him to recognize the grace of God on his ministry and to be strong in it. "Thou therefore, my son, be strong in the grace that is in Christ Jesus" (2 Timothy 2:1).

Paul spoke about how *he* recognized the grace of God on *his* life. He had recognized the grace of God on Timothy and had asked him to be strong in that grace. But he was able to recognize the grace of God on his own ministry and this made him work even harder. He said he laboured even more abundantly because of this grace. When you recognise the grace of God you must jump into action and work harder than ever.

> But by the grace of God I am what I am: and his grace which *was bestowed* upon me was not in vain; but I laboured more abundantly than they all: yet not I, but the grace of God which was with me.
>
> 1 Corinthians 15:10

1.   *RECOGNIZE THE GRACE OF GOD THAT BRINGS SUPERNATURAL MIRACLES.*

Supernatural events can turn the tide in your life and

change you from a struggling, poverty-stricken brother to a prosperous mogul. Elijah survived by the supernatural provision of the ravens. ("Get thee hence, and turn thee eastward, and hide thyself by the brook Cherith, that is before Jordan. And it shall be, that thou shalt drink of the brook; and I have commanded the ravens to feed thee there. So he went and did according unto the word of the LORD: for he went and dwelt by the brook Cherith, that is before Jordan. And the ravens brought him bread and flesh in the morning, and bread and flesh in the evening; and he drank of the brook" (1 Kings 17:3-6).

The miracles that I have experienced in my ministry have greatly enhanced my life and given me more visibility and acceptability. My ministry moved to a higher level when I moved into the ministry of miracles, signs and wonders. Whether you like it or not, miracles cause crowds to throng to a minister. You will be surprised about how God will prosper you and your ministry when you accept what supernatural miracles can do for you.

2. *RECOGNIZE THE GRACE OF GOD THAT HAS GIVEN YOU CERTAIN GIFTS.*

You can also become prosperous through gifts. Our pride tells us that we must earn everything we have. We love to boast about how hard we worked to get the things we have. But God may want to make you rich through gifts that He expects you to receive. I have enjoyed many gifts in my life and ministry. For several years, I used cars that were given to me as gifts. I could not afford a car but I prospered through gifts given to me. Solomon, the new king, received gifts which became a blessing to him. Indeed, Solomon prospered because of the gifts that he received. Solomon received gifts of timber from Hiram, his father's friend. The queen of Sheba also gave gifts to Solomon. Indeed, Solomon became rich through the gifts he received.

> And Hiram sent to Solomon, saying, I have considered the things which thou sentest to me for: and I will do all thy desire concerning timber of cedar, and concerning timber of fir.

> My servants shall bring them down from Lebanon unto the sea: and I will convey them by sea in floats unto the place that thou shalt appoint me, and will cause them to be discharged there, and thou shalt receive them: and thou shalt accomplish my desire, in giving food for my household.

> So Hiram gave Solomon cedar trees and fir trees according to all his desire.

1 Kings 5:8-10

> And she gave the king an hundred and twenty talents of gold, and of spices great abundance, and precious stones: neither was there any such spice as the queen of Sheba gave king Solomon.

> And the servants also of Huram, and the servants of Solomon, which brought gold from Ophir, brought algum trees and precious stones.

> And the king made of the algum trees terraces to the house of the Lord, and to the king's palace, and harps and psalteries for singers: and there were none such seen before in the land of Judah.

2 Chronicles 9:9-11

3. *RECOGNIZE THE GRACE OF GOD THAT HAS GIVEN YOU A PARTICULAR PROFESSION.*

And because he was of the same craft, he abode with them, and wrought: for by their occupation THEY WERE TENTMAKERS.

Acts 18:3

Unfortunately, having been to school and learning a profession does not guarantee a job today. Because many of us cannot think outside the possibility of our learned profession, we often miss the numerous other ways by which God makes provision for our prosperity.

This book is intended to open your eyes to see the other possible ways by which God can bring you into prosperity. This is what the Lord said to Adam. "...Behold, I have given you every plant yielding seed that is on the surface of all the earth, and every tree which has fruit yielding seed; it shall be food for you..." (Genesis 1:29, NASB). This is what the Lord is saying to us today.

Open your eyes.

Look around and you will see that I have made a provision for you to prosper.

May the Lord open your eyes to see several different ways by which prosperity can come into your hands!

4. *RECOGNIZE THE GRACE OF GOD THAT COMES THROUGH YOUR MINISTRY.*

Even so hath the Lord ordained that they which preach the gospel should live of the gospel.

1 Corinthians 9:14

Obeying the call of God can help you to prosper. God has ordained that preachers should live from their calling to the ministry. Many people think that priests should have nothing because they do "nothing". But these are the thoughts of an ignoramus. Not allowing hard-working priests to prosper would violate the law of sowing and reaping. Why should a priest sow seeds only to be told he should not harvest anything?

Modern priests seem to be quite the opposite of biblical priests. Some modern priests have cars, houses and wealth. Because of this, modern pastors are criticised for being charlatans and hypocrites.

A close look at the laws of Moses will reveal that the Levites were to *receive no portion* of the land from the conquest of the Promised Land. However, a closer look at the Law of Moses revealed how the Levites actually owned lands that were given to them by the people (from the Lord).

The Scripture clearly shows that Levites actually owned land and cattle. It was how they came about owning land that was different. The Levites (priests, pastors, reverends, bishops) were to have forty-eight cities in all. They were to have pasturelands for their livestock. This shows that the Levites actually had land, cities and livestock. Please do not be upset when you see that the Lord has given some pastors lands, cities, herds and flocks.

Now the Lord spoke to Moses in the plains of Moab by the Jordan opposite Jericho, saying,

> "Command the sons of Israel that they give to the Levites from the inheritance of their possession, cities to live in; and you shall give to the Levites pasture lands around the cities.

THE CITIES SHALL BE *THEIRS* TO LIVE IN; AND THEIR PASTURE LANDS SHALL BE FOR *THEIR CATTLE* AND FOR *THEIR HERDS* AND FOR ALL *THEIR BEASTS.*

"And the pasture lands of the cities which you shall give to the Levites shall extend from the wall of the city outward a thousand cubits around.

You shall also measure outside the city on the east side two thousand cubits, and on the south side two thousand cubits, and on the west side two thousand cubits, and on the north side two thousand cubits, with the city in the center. THIS SHALL BECOME THEIRS as pasture lands for the cities.

The cities which you shall give to the Levites shall be the six cities of refuge, which you shall give for the manslayer to flee to; and in addition to them you shall give forty-two cities.

All the cities which you shall give to the Levites shall be forty-eight cities, together with their pasture lands.

Numbers 35:1-7 (NASB)

5. RECOGNIZE THE GRACE OF GOD THAT HAS GIVEN YOU SPECIALISED KNOWLEDGE.

There were some young Israeli men who enjoyed life at the king's palace because of the special knowledge and wisdom they had. Perhaps, God has given you a special ability to play the piano or to play golf or to speak a particular language. You will be surprised to find out that God has intended to bless you through this special skill and knowledge.

And the king spake unto Ashpenaz the master of his eunuchs, that he should bring certain of the children of Israel, and of the king's seed, and of the princes;

Children in whom was no blemish, but well favoured, and SKILFUL IN ALL WISDOM, and CUNNING IN KNOWLEDGE, and UNDERSTANDING SCIENCE, and such as had ability in them to stand in the king's palace, and whom they might teach the learning and the tongue of the Chaldeans.

And the king appointed them a daily provision of the king's meat, and of the wine which he drank: so nourishing them three years, that at the end thereof they might stand before the king.

Now among these were of the children of Judah, Daniel, Hananiah, Mishael, and Azariah:

Daniel 1:3-6

6. *RECOGNIZE THE GRACE OF GOD THAT ENABLES YOU TO PROSPER THROUGH SOMETHING THAT YOU WERE NOT TRAINED FOR.*

Prosperity may not come through what you learned in school. Accept this fact quickly and open yourself to God's provision. Jesus was trained to be a carpenter "Is not this the carpenter, the son of Mary...?" (Mark 6:3) but He became a minister of the gospel. His needs were not met by the carpentry trade. His needs were met by the way all ministers' needs are met – through gifts, offerings and substance ministered unto Him by the people.

And Joanna the wife of Chuza Herod's steward, and Susanna, and many others, which ministered unto him of their substance.

Luke 8:3

Most successful people that I know worked in areas that they were not trained for. I was trained to be a medical doctor but I do not live by the practice of medicine. I am sustained through the ministry. Most of the presidents I know of were trained in different fields but are sustained by politics. In one presidential election, I could count six medical doctors including heart surgeons who wanted to be presidents of Ghana. Their desire to be presidents is not wrong. It is just another example of how people are trained for one thing and yet prosper through something else.

7.   *RECOGNIZE THE GRACE OF GOD THAT HAS GIVEN YOU PARTICULAR ABILITIES.*

God may give you a special ability to do certain things. You may be able to sing, you may be able to paint or you may be able to play instruments. These are all special abilities God may have given you. If you recognize that the grace of God has given you special abilities, you will nurture them and prosper through them. You will be able to receive God's grace to prosper. Notice this interesting story of someone who used his artistic ability to escape and prosper.

The Freedom of the Artist

One day, for amusement, the Italian Renaissance painter Fra Filippo Lippi (1406 – 1469) and some friends went sailing in a small boat off Ancona. There they were captured by two

Moorish galleys, which hauled them off in chains to Barbary where they were sold as slaves. For eighteen long months Filippo toiled with no hope of returning to Italy.

On several occasions Filippo saw the man who had brought him pass by, and one day he decided to sketch this man's portrait, using burnt coal – charcoal – from the fire. Still in his chains he found a white wall where he drew a full-length likeness of his owner in Moorish clothing. The owner soon heard about this, for no one had seen such skill in drawing before in these parts. It seemed like a miracle, a gift from God. The drawing so pleased the owner that he instantly gave Filippo his freedom and employed him in his court. All the big men on the Barbary coast came to see the magnificent colour portraits that Fra Filippo then proceeded to do, and finally, in gratitude for the honour in this way brought upon him, Filippo's owner returned the artist safely to Italy.

Like Fra Filippo (if to a lesser degree) most of us possess some gift, some talent, an ability to do something better than other people. Use your talent as a stepping stone. Your God-given "special ability" may buy your freedom and give you the prosperity and blessing that you need.

There are people whose main gift is in their carefulness, their tact, their diplomacy, their prudence and their maturity.

God may bless you with a particular skill. You must learn to use these skills in order to prosper. Your prosperity may not come through your education but through a skill God has blessed you with. The children of Judah were endowed with skills that set them apart.

And the king spake unto Ashpenaz the master of his eunuchs, that he should bring certain of the children of Israel, and of the king's seed, and of the princes;

Children in whom was no blemish, but well favoured, and skilful in all wisdom, and cunning in knowledge, and understanding science, and SUCH AS HAD ABILITY in them to stand in the king's palace, and whom they might teach the learning and the tongue of the Chaldeans.

And the king appointed them a daily provision of the king's meat, and of the wine which he drank: so nourishing them three years, that at the end thereof they might stand before the king.

Now among these were of the children of Judah, Daniel, Hananiah, Mishael, and Azariah:

Daniel 1:3-6

8.   *RECOGNIZE THE GRACE OF GOD THAT HAS MADE YOU BEAUTIFUL.*

Now when the turn of Esther, the daughter of Abihail the uncle of Mordecai, who had taken her for his daughter, was come to go in unto the king, she required nothing but what Hegai the king's chamberlain, the keeper of the women, appointed. And ESTHER OBTAINED FAVOUR IN THE SIGHT OF ALL THEM THAT LOOKED UPON HER.

So Esther was taken unto king Ahasuerus into his house royal in the tenth month, which is the month Tebeth, in the seventh year of his reign.

And the king loved Esther above all the women, and she obtained grace and favour in his sight more than all the virgins; so that he set the royal crown upon her head, and made her queen instead of Vashti.

Esther 2:15-17

Whether you like it or not, your appearance affects the favour you come into. Many people are hired because of what they look like. You may not want to accept that but it is a fact, even in the church.

Anyone who does not take their appearance seriously is not taking their prosperity seriously. You can have jobs that belong to a more qualified person if you take your appearance more seriously. There are many jobs a more qualified person could do. You must consider your beauty as an important asset given to you by the Lord to help open doors for your life.

It is no secret that fat people are considered to be lazy, slow, too old, undisciplined and lacking self-control. This perception may be wrong but it is a generalized pervading perception.

It is time you took your appearance seriously. Being too fat may not just cost you extra material for a larger coat but it may actually cost you your job.

9. *RECOGNIZE THE GRACE OF GOD THAT MAKES SOMEONE KIND TO YOU.*

Give, and it shall be given unto you; good measure, pressed down, and shaken together, and running over, shall men give into your bosom. For with the same measure that ye mete withal it shall be measured to you again.

Luke 6:38

Not everybody shows kindness. Most people are full of cruelty. God will send people who will show you kindness and favour. God can provide for you through the kindness and compassion of others. One of the famous laws of Moses reveals the mind of Jehovah. God expects those that are rich to allow their riches to affect the less fortunate around them. God does not expect the rich to be miserly and calculating when dealing with poor people. "When you reap the harvest of your land, don't reap the corners of your field or gather the gleanings. Leave them for the poor and the foreigners. I am God, your God" (Leviticus 23:22, The Message: The Bible in Contemporary Language).

They are to overlook many things and allow the poor to benefit. They are to act as though they do not know about all their rightful possessions. They are to act as though they do not notice that some of their profits are lost. God has a mind to prosper poor people through the excessive riches of blessed people.

10. *RECOGNIZE THE GRACE OF GOD THAT GIVES YOU FAVOUR.*

Favour is when someone likes you without any good reason. You can prosper because someone looks upon you favourably. Esther was one amongst thousands of available and willing ladies, yet she was chosen. Why? What did she have that others did not have? The answer is "favour."

So Esther was taken unto king Ahasuerus into his house royal in the tenth month, which is the month Tebeth, in the seventh year of his reign.

And the king loved Esther above all the women, and SHE OBTAINED GRACE AND FAVOUR in his sight more than all the virgins; so that he set the royal crown upon her head, and made her queen instead of Vashti.

Esther 2:16-17

11. RECOGNIZE THE GRACE OF GOD THAT HAS GIVEN YOU AN UNDERSTANDING OF COMPLEX ISSUES.

Deep calleth unto deep at the noise of thy waterspouts: all thy waves and thy billows are gone over me.

Psalm 42:7

The ability to understand what is happening can also generate wealth. Every leader looks for people who have a certain depth of reasoning. Whenever they find someone who can reason along certain lines they promote the fellow and relate more closely to him. Scripture teaches us that "deep calls unto deep." *Leaders are deep and they relate with people who are equally deep.* The deep leader calls out to someone who is equally deep. King David had a friend called Ahithophel with whom he had sweet, deep fellowship. King Solomon had a friend called Zabud. Both Ahitophel and Zabud must have been deep enough to relate with the kings.

12. RECOGNIZE THE GRACE OF GOD THAT MAKES YOU OCCUPY A SPECIAL POSITION.

For a day in thy courts is better than a thousand. I had rather be a doorkeeper in the house of my God, than to dwell in the tents of wickedness.

Psalm 84:10

The position you occupy can become a great source of prosperity. David recognized this when he said he would prefer to be a doorkeeper in the house of the Lord than to live in tents of wickedness.

It is important to recognize what God has chosen to use to bless you with. Sometimes you have a position that is more important strategically than the job itself.

Like Nehemiah, you may be the secretary to the king. The job of a secretary itself may not be that prestigious but being the secretary to the king may hold greater prospects than being the manager of a bank. Sometimes, the position becomes more important than the job itself. Being the head of an ant is still smaller than being the tail of the elephant.

Recognize when God blesses you through strategic positioning. Flow in the position that God has granted you and make the most of it. It may be the door to all the blessings of your life.

And it came to pass in the month Nisan, in the twentieth year of Artaxerxes the king, that wine was before him: and I took up the wine, and gave it unto the king. Now I had not been beforetime sad in his presence...

Then the king said unto me, for what dost thou make request? So I prayed to the God of heaven.

And I said unto the king, If it please the king, and if thy servant have found favour in thy sight, that thou wouldest send me unto Judah, unto the city of my fathers' sepulchres, that I may build it.

Nehemiah 2:1,4-5

13.   *RECOGNIZE THE GRACE OF GOD THAT COMES TO YOU THROUGH NATURE.*

This is the oldest way by which men become prosperous. Through the animals He has created, men get food to eat.

Through the plants God created, the sons of men get food to eat. In primitive societies, people rarely go beyond the gift of nature all around them. They simply depend on creation and what it has to offer: they harvest the plants God created; they kill and eat the animals that God put on the earth; they mine gold, copper, manganese, diamonds they discover in their soil; and finally they drill the oil they find under the ocean on their coast.

This is the most basic form of God's provision and it is used basically in the third world. People who major in this kind of provision are usually poor.

And God said, BEHOLD, I HAVE GIVEN YOU EVERY HERB BEARING SEED, which is upon the face of all the earth, and every tree...

Genesis 1:29

14.   *RECOGNIZE THE GRACE OF GOD THAT COMES TO YOU THROUGH THE CHURCH OF GOD.*

And the multitude of them that believed were of one heart and of one soul: neither said any of them that ought of the things which he possessed was his own; but they had all things common. And with great power gave the apostles witness of the resurrection of the Lord Jesus: and great grace was upon them all. NEITHER WAS THERE ANY AMONG THEM THAT LACKED: for as many as were possessors of lands or houses sold them, and brought the prices of the things that were sold,

Acts 4:32-34

The Scripture above shows how many people were sustained by the church. In Ghana, during the famine of 1983, the nation was greatly helped by the Catholic Church. Through the Catholic Relief Services, many people in the nation received food and supplies.

Indeed, you can also be blessed by and through your church. A church is a place to receive spiritual impartation. The church is not a source of jobs or loans. However, God has also blessed certain people through the church. Some people have found prosperity by being in or associated with a church.

15.   *RECOGNIZE THE GRACE OF GOD THAT COMES TO YOU THROUGH YOUR INHERITANCE.*

Indeed, God may give you all that you need through your inheritance. Isaac became rich because his father gave him all his possessions.

And ABRAHAM GAVE ALL THAT HE HAD UNTO ISAAC.

But unto the sons of the concubines, which Abraham had, Abraham gave gifts, and sent them away from Isaac his son, while he yet lived, eastward, unto the east country.

And these are the days of the years of Abraham's life which he lived, an hundred threescore and fifteen years.

Genesis 25:5-7

Chapter 9

"He That Hath"
Will Get Even More
Because He Is a Builder

Seven Reasons Why It Is Biblical
to Build Houses

1. **Jesus taught that it was odd for foxes and birds to have homes whilst a man did not have a home.** He taught us that foxes are to have holes, birds to have nests and men are to have houses.

    And Jesus said unto him, Foxes have holes, and birds of the air have nests; but the Son of man hath not where to lay his head.

    Luke 9:58

2. The Bible teaches how a good shepherd leads his sheep to the most appropriate dwelling place. The most appropriate dwelling place for a sheep is the green pasture and the most appropriate dwelling place for a human being is a house.

He maketh me to lie down in green pastures: he leadeth me beside the still waters.

Psalms 23:2

3. The Bible teaches on the need for Christians to give houses to their children as an inheritance. If you do not have a house how can you leave an inheritance of a house for your children? How can you be a good father and leave an inheritance for your children if you do not have a house?

House and riches are the inheritance of fathers: and a prudent wife is from the Lord.

Proverbs 19:14

4. In times past, God has spoken through His prophets, directing His people to build houses for themselves.

Build ye houses, and dwell in them; and plant gardens, and eat the fruit of them;

Jeremiah 29:5

5. The ability to build a house is described as a specific blessing that came from God.

And it came to pass, because the midwives feared God, that he made them houses.

Exodus 1:21

6. **The ability to build houses is seen as a fruit of God's wisdom.** If you fill yourself with God's wisdom you will be able to build a house.

Through wisdom is an house builded; and by understanding it is established:

Proverbs 24:3

7. **Jesus said He would give His disciples houses as a reward for following Him.**

And Jesus answered and said, Verily I say unto you, There is no man that hath left house, or brethren, or sisters, or father, or mother, or wife, or children, or lands, for my sake, and the gospel's, But he shall receive an hundredfold now in this time, HOUSES, and brethren, and sisters, and mothers, and children, and lands, with persecutions; and in the world to come eternal life.

Mark 10:29-30

Why Rich People Build Houses

1. **Rich people make it an early priority to build a house. Rich people discern the season for building.** Very few people in this world ever build houses for themselves. One of the reasons they do not build houses is because they constantly wait for the right season of their lives to build. But the best time to build a house is now. There has never been, and there will never be enough money. Now is the best time to build and rich people always build now.

A time to kill, and a time to heal; a time to break down, AND A TIME TO BUILD UP;

Ecclesiastes 3:3

2. Rich people build houses because they do not follow fantasies.

He that tilleth his land shall have plenty of bread: but he that followeth after vain persons shall have poverty enough.

Proverbs 28:19

Rich people do not follow imaginary high-sounding ideas. There are people who are full of schemes, projections and plans. They can speak for hours on end about their proposals and what they think will work. Such people do not usually accomplish much for themselves. Such people never build houses.

You simply need to roll up your sleeves and get to the job. People who plan for years to travel abroad instead of going to the school that is nearby often do not amount to much.

3. Rich people build houses because they do not follow pleasures.

He that loveth pleasure shall be a poor man: he that loveth wine and oil shall not be rich.

Proverbs 21:17

Lovers of pleasure cannot build houses. Pleasure is expensive and lots of money is needed to have a "good time". Houses are equally expensive and require the heaviest investment of your money. People who love the pleasure of wining and dining, wearing expensive clothes, driving expensive cars will simply not have the money to build a house. The cost of these luxuries amounts to the cost of a house. In fact, there are many cars that are more expensive than a house. Often, you have to choose between enjoying yourself and owning a house. Rich people choose to build houses rather than spending their money on fleeting luxuries.

4. Rich people build houses because they are frugal.

Frugality is the key to building a house. Rich people build houses because they are frugal. Frugal people are constantly saving money. They do not want to waste anything no matter how much they have.

It is interesting to note that poor nations waste their water resources by allowing most of the water they generate to go waste.

Poor people waste their money by leaving lights and electric gadgets on when they do not need them.

Poor nations waste their human resources by driving away the most skilled and wealthy people.

5. Rich people build houses because they pray for wisdom.

It is difficult to believe that money is not the key ingredient for building a house. Building is impossible for most people. That is why you need the wisdom that makes you overcome impossible things. My eighty-year-old father-in-law once said: "A house is built by wisdom and not by money." He built many houses in his lifetime so he should know a thing or two about building houses. But Solomon had said it already. He said:

Through wisdom is an house builded; and by understanding it is established: And by knowledge shall the chambers be filled with all precious and pleasant riches.

Proverbs 24:3-4

6. Rich people build their own houses after they build God's house.

People who become rich understand the importance of priorities. God's house comes before your own house. Solomon, the richest man in the world built God's house before he built his own house. The experience that he gathered whilst building God's house was used to build his own house.

Building God's house will be a step to building your own house.

But Solomon was building his own house thirteen years, and HE FINISHED ALL HIS HOUSE.

1 Kings 7:1

7. Rich people build houses because they know it is the best investment for their money.

When people have a little money they often do not know what to do with it. They often put it in the wrong place. Most people do the wrong things with the money that they have. Most of us do not understand what the word *'real estate'* really means. There are many unreal estates. These unreal estates can collapse overnight and turn a wealthy man into a pauper. The good and real estate on this earth is property.

8. Rich people build houses because they use what God has provided for them.

God has provided for everyone. He has provided something for you and with that you will be able to accomplish something for yourself.

Instead of continuously fretting and concerning yourself

with what you do not have, look around and see what God has given you. He may not have given you what He has given others. But He has given you something.

And God said, Behold, I have given you every herb bearing seed, which is upon the face of all the earth, and every tree, in the which is the fruit of a tree yielding seed; to you it shall be for meat.

Genesis 1:29

9. Rich people build houses because they have the humility to build slowly like the man who built on a rock.

Obviously, building on sand would be much quicker than building on a rock. In fact, it would take a long time to build a foundation on a rock. Proper construction takes a long time. You must be prepared to spend a long time building your house. You must not expect things to be completed in a short time.

There is a type of man who simply wants to rent a house now. He does not want to roll up his sleeves and build anything. He wants to look successful and accomplished *today*. Looking successful, accomplished and settled costs people true prosperity. The price of looking successful and accomplished quickly is often the price of a house.

He is like a man which built an house, and digged deep, and laid the foundation on a rock: and when the flood arose, the stream beat vehemently upon that house, and could not shake it: for it was founded upon a rock.

Luke 6:48

10. **Rich people build houses because they are pragmatic.**
You may plan to live in a mansion way up on a hill. But you may not be able to practically build your dream house. You need to be realistic and do what you can do for now. Step by step you will rise on the property ladder. And God will take you from victory to victory and glory to glory. Life is such that you do not have what you really want. You often cannot drive the car you really like or live in a house you really like. Also, most people are not married to the kind of person they would really like. Those who wait for the "ideal" never enter into the "real".

You will never have the money that you really need. Most people will never really be able to employ a contractor. Many people will have to fight the problems of life and build a house at the same time. If you are waiting for a good time when everything is okay and money is flowing you may never build anything. Nehemiah had to fight and build at the same time.

Those who were REBUILDING the wall and those who carried burdens took *their* load WITH ONE HAND DOING THE WORK AND THE OTHER HOLDING A WEAPON.

Nehemiah 4:17, NASB

11. **Rich people build houses because they are able to work for long hours.**

Nehemiah worked for long hours. Many rich people work for long hours. The principle is the same. If you sow seeds for many hours you would have sown many more seeds than someone who sowed for a few hours. Obviously, you will reap much more by working longer hours. Rich people work for long hours and this enables them to build houses. Nehemiah built the wall from dawn until the stars appeared.

SO WE LABOURED IN THE WORK: AND HALF OF THEM HELD THE SPEARS FROM THE RISING OF THE MORNING TILL THE STARS APPEARED.

Likewise at the same time said I unto the people, Let every one with his servant lodge within Jerusalem, that in the night they may be a guard to us, and labour on the day.

So neither I, nor my brethren, nor my servants, nor the men of the guard which followed me, NONE OF US PUT OFF OUR CLOTHES, SAVING THAT EVERY ONE PUT THEM OFF FOR WASHING.

Nehemiah 4:21-23

12. Rich people build houses because they do many jobs at the same time.

Nehemiah, who built the walls of Jerusalem, deployed the principle of doing many jobs at the same time. Many rich people do several jobs at the same time. After all, the principle is clear: You reap what you sow. If you sow into many jobs you will reap from many jobs.

So we laboured in the work: and half of them held the spears from the rising of the morning till the stars appeared.

Likewise at the same time said I unto the people, Let every one with his servant lodge within Jerusalem, THAT IN THE NIGHT THEY MAY BE A GUARD TO US, AND LABOUR ON THE DAY.

So neither I, nor my brethren, nor my servants, nor the men of the guard which followed me, none of us put off our clothes, saving that every one put them off for washing.

Nehemiah 4:21-23

13. Rich people build houses because they work in the day as well as in the night.

Nehemiah, who built Jerusalem, worked in the day as well as in the night. Working in the day as well as in the night enables you to sow important seeds that will bear fruit. The seeds sown in the day and the seeds sown in the night will combine to give you a mighty harvest. It is this harvest that will be used to build a great house.

So we laboured in the work: and half of them held the spears from the rising of the morning till the stars appeared.

Likewise at the same time said I unto the people, Let every one with his servant lodge within Jerusalem, THAT IN THE NIGHT THEY MAY BE A GUARD TO US, AND LABOUR ON THE DAY.

Nehemiah 4:21-22

Chapter 10

"He That Hath"
Will Get Even More Because
He is a Sower of Seeds

Why Sowing Seeds Makes People Rich

1.   **Sowing seeds makes people rich because seeds are God's creation to provide wealth in the earth. God is the inventor of seeds.**

And God said, Let the earth bring forth grass, the herb yielding seed, and the fruit tree yielding fruit after his kind, whose seed is in itself, upon the earth: and it was so.

And the earth brought forth grass, and herb yielding seed after his kind, and the tree yielding fruit, whose seed was in itself, after his kind: and God saw that it was good.

Genesis 1:11-12

God's creation is loaded with seeds. God created living things to have seeds within them. These seeds are the oldest source of wealth in the world. Anyone who needs corn just has to plant some seeds and he will have the harvest of corn with its resultant wealth. Seed planting is therefore the basis of God's continued provision of wealth for us.

Next time you are flying across the rich western world, make sure you look out of the window. You will notice that the fields are divided into squares and rectangles. This picture of squares and rectangles is the picture you get by looking at rich European countries who have planted seeds on every available space. However, when you fly over poor undeveloped countries, you will notice that there are no such squares and rectangles. This is because the land has been left largely unused. There is a lot of bush, savannah and unused virgin forest. The rich get richer because they planted many seeds. The poor get poorer because they have not planted anything. How can poor countries expect to have rice when they have planted no rice?

"He that hath" respects the principle of sowing seeds.

2.   Sowing seeds gives you the legal right to a harvest. Sowing seeds makes people rich because every wise planter of seeds is entitled to a harvest.

Sowing seeds makes people rich because *life is made up of harvest sessions that come after seed planting sessions.* "He that hath" has faithfully done his seed planting sessions. He is entitled to harvest sessions.

While the earth remaineth, seedtime and harvest, and
cold and heat, and summer and winter, and day and
night shall not cease.

Genesis 8:22

3. Good things are seeds. Sowing seeds makes people rich because the "seed nature" is also deeply embedded in good things.

Let him that is taught in the word communicate unto
him that teacheth in all GOOD THINGS. Be not
deceived; God is not mocked: for whatsoever a man
soweth, that shall he also reap,

Galatians 6:6-7

The Bible teaches us that whatsoever a man sows will be
reaped. It did not specify what the 'whatsoever' stands for.
This means that many things can be 'sowed' and 'reaped'.

*Inanimate objects which are good things contain seed
power.*

I once gave away a precious walkman that was my precious
music station. Some years later, someone gave me a large
sound system with powerful speakers. The Lord reminded
me that I had sowed my precious walkman in obedience to
His instructions. If you give away some clothes or food,
expect to receive a harvest. Food and clothes are good things
and whatsoever you sow will be reaped.

If you sow a house, you can expect to reap houses. If you
sow a car you can expect to reap cars. Houses are good things
and cars are good things. "He that hath" sows good things.

4. **Spiritual virtues are seeds that can be sown. Sowing seeds makes people have more good things because the "seed nature" is embedded in spiritual virtues. For instance, sowing mercy and being merciful causes you to reap a harvest of mercy.**

Then his lord, after that he had called him, said unto him, O thou wicked servant, I forgave thee all that debt, because thou desiredst me:

Shouldest not thou also have had compassion on thy fellowservant, even as I had pity on thee?

And his lord was wroth, and delivered him to the tormentors, till he should pay all that was due unto him.

So likewise shall my heavenly Father do also unto you, if ye from your hearts forgive not every one his brother their trespasses.

Matthew 18:32-35

When the servant did not forgive his fellow servant, he reaped a harvest of sorrow, imprisonment and impoverishment. If he had sown mercy he would have reaped a harvest of mercy.

Blessed *are* the merciful: for they shall obtain mercy.

Matthew 5:7

David sowed a seed of honour and loyalty by sparing the life of Saul; and reaped a harvest when his life was spared by the mighty men. "And he said unto his men, The LORD forbid that I should do this thing unto my master, the LORD'S anointed, to stretch forth mine hand against him, seeing he is the anointed of the LORD" (1 Samuel 24:6).

5. Good deeds are seeds that can be sown. Every good thing you do to somebody will come back as a harvest of good things for you.

Knowing that whatsoever good thing any man doeth, the same shall he receive of the Lord, whether he be bond or free.

Ephesians 6:8

The key in this Scripture is to *not expect the harvest from a human being* but from the Lord. Human beings who receive your seeds will not usually have the ability to pay you back.

Whatever you sow as a good deed or kindness will become a blessing to you one day. If you counsel someone's child and care for him as your own, you can expect to receive a harvest of good counsel, care and love from the Lord. If you look after someone's children you can expect your children to be looked after.

6. The Word of God is a seed that can be sown.

The sower soweth the word.

Mark 4:14

You may wonder how the Word of God can generate prosperity. Because the Word of God is God's wisdom, every time you receive the Word of God, you sow wisdom into your life. Wisdom, the Bible says, gives rise to prosperity.

Happy is the man that findeth wisdom, and the man that getteth understanding.

For the merchandise of it is better than the merchandise of silver, and the gain thereof than fine gold. She is more precious than rubies: and all the things thou canst desire are not to be compared unto her.

Length of days is in her right hand; AND IN HER LEFT HAND RICHES AND HONOUR.

Proverbs 3:13-16

If the Word of God is a seed then a book about the Word of God, a sermon on the Word of God, a TV program on the Word of God, a CD or DVD on the Word of God is also a seed.

You must sow the Word of God into your own life and reap the harvest of a good life and prosperity.

7.   Money is a seed that can be sown.

The Bible also teaches us that money is a seed. The Bible describes giving money to God as sowing a seed. If you need some money all you have to do is to sow some money seeds and you will receive a harvest of money. Paul the apostle described money as a seed.

But this I say, He which SOWETH sparingly shall reap also sparingly; and he which SOWETH bountifully shall reap also bountifully. Every man according as he purposeth in his heart, so let him GIVE; not grudgingly, or of necessity: for God loveth a cheerful GIVER. And God is able to make all grace abound toward you; that ye, always having all sufficiency in all things, may abound to every good work:

2 Corinthians 9:6-9

8.   The tithe is a *special seed* that can be sown.

This special seed, entitles you to a harvest of open heavens. This special seed entitles you to have the devourer rebuked.

> Bring ye all the tithes into the storehouse, that there may be meat in mine house, and prove me now herewith, saith the Lord of hosts, if I will not open you the windows of heaven, and pour you out a blessing, that there shall not be room enough to receive it.
>
> Malachi 3:10

9.   A seed to the poor is a *special seed* that gives a harvest of preservation, long life, health, and deliverance from enemies.   Read it for yourself and see the blessings that are promised when you sow seeds into the life of a poor person.

> Blessed is he that considereth the poor: the Lord will deliver him in time of trouble. *The Lord will preserve him,* and *keep him alive;* and *he shall be blessed* upon the earth: and *thou wilt not deliver him unto the will of his enemies. The Lord will strengthen* him upon the bed of languishing: thou wilt *make all his bed* in his sickness.
>
> Psalms 41:1-3

10.   A seed of money mixed with prayer is a special seed that gives a harvest of a spiritual visitation.

Cornelius sowed a special combined seed of alms and prayer. This seed came up to God as a memorial. I didn't write the Bible. The Bible says that the angel told Cornelius that his gifts and prayers had become a memorial in Heaven. This memorial reminded God about Cornelius on a daily basis. This is why the angel was sent to visit Cornelius. Your special seed of prayer and alms can provoke a spiritual visitation for your life.

> There was a certain man in Caesarea called Cornelius, a centurion of the band called the Italian band,
>
> A devout man, and one that feared God with all his house, which gave much alms to the people, and prayed to God alway.
>
> He saw in a vision evidently about the ninth hour of the day an angel of God coming in to him, and saying unto him, Cornelius.
>
> And when he looked on him, he was afraid, and said, What is it, Lord? And he said unto him, THY PRAYERS AND THINE ALMS are come up for A MEMORIAL before God.
>
> Acts 10:1-4

11. A seed towards evangelism and missions is a *special seed* that will cause God to provide all your needs according to His riches.

A seed was sent to support the Apostle Paul in his mission. Paul pronounced the special blessing of Philippians 4:19 on them.

This verse is commonly quoted by people who claim God will care for them. But the proclamation of Philippians 4:19 was the harvest of the seed sown into Paul's evangelistic mission. Remember that your special seed towards evangelism will entitle you to a special harvest of abundant all-round provision.

> You yourselves also know, Philippians, that at the first preaching of the gospel, AFTER I LEFT MACEDONIA, NO CHURCH SHARED WITH ME IN THE MATTER OF GIVING AND RECEIVING BUT YOU ALONE;
>
> for even in Thessalonica you sent a gift more than once for my needs.
>
> Not that I seek the gift itself, but I seek for the profit which increases to your account.
>
> But I have received everything in full and have an abundance; I am amply supplied, having received from Epaphroditus what you have sent, a fragrant aroma, an acceptable sacrifice, well-pleasing to God.
>
> And my God will supply all your needs according to His riches in glory in Christ Jesus.
>
> Philippians 4:15-19 (NASB)

12.   A seed to your spiritual teacher is a *special seed* that fulfils righteousness.

Through this special seed you fulfil all righteousness and complete certain spiritual contracts. Because there is a clear and biblical instruction to minister to your teacher, every time you do so, you fulfil the command to play your part in your teacher's life, paying him back for his good works in your life. You fulfil your obligation as a good student and receive the blessings of Galatians 6:7.

Let him that is taught in the word communicate unto him that teacheth in all good things. Be not deceived; God is not mocked: for whatsoever a man soweth, that shall he also reap.

Galatians 6:6-7

13. "Helping somebody" is a special seed that can be sown.

Knowing that whatsoever good thing any man doeth, the same shall he receive of the Lord, whether he be bond or free.

Ephesians 6:8

Without help you will not make it in life. You will need assistance, forgiveness, mercy, a push, favour and, above all, undeserved help. Many do not sow this seed of help, because people who receive help from you do not look like they could ever return the favour shown them. But you must expect your harvest from God and not from the person you helped. Do not look to the person you are helping as the source of your harvest.

Five People Who Sowed a Special Seed by Helping Others

1. Rahab sowed a seed of 'help' by helping the spies and she reaped it when they later helped her to escape death.

Now therefore, I pray you, swear unto me by the LORD, since I have shewed you kindness, that ye will also shew kindness unto my father's house, and give me a true token:

And that ye will save alive my father, and my mother, and my brethren, and my sisters, and all that they have, and deliver our lives from death.

And the men answered her, Our life for yours, if ye utter not this our business. And it shall be, when the LORD hath given us the land, that we will deal kindly and truly with thee.

Joshua 2:12-14

2. Onesiphorus sowed a seed of 'help' when he helped Paul and reaped a harvest when Paul blessed him to receive mercy.

The Lord give mercy unto the house of Onesiphorus; for he oft refreshed me, and was not ashamed of my chain:

2 Timothy 1:16

3. Joseph sowed a seed of 'help' when he helped the butler to interpret his dream and reaped a harvest when the butler recommended him to Pharaoh.

And there was there with us a young man, an Hebrew, servant to the captain of the guard; and we told him, and he interpreted to us our dreams; to each man according to his dream he did interpret.

And it came to pass, as he interpreted to us, so it was; me he restored unto mine office, and him he hanged.

Then Pharaoh sent and called Joseph, and they brought him hastily out of the dungeon: and he shaved himself, and changed his raiment, and came in unto Pharaoh.

Genesis 41:12-14

4.   The disciples sowed seeds of 'help' by continuing with Jesus in His ministry and are promised a harvest in Heaven.

Ye are they which have continued with me in my temptations. And I appoint unto you a kingdom, as my Father hath appointed unto me; that ye may eat and drink at my table in my kingdom, and sit on thrones judging the twelve tribes of Israel.

Luke 22:28-36

5.   Abigail sows a seed of 'help' when she helps a man of God and reaps a harvest when she gets a husband soon after being widowed.

Abigail sent food to David. It was a great blessing to David and his men in their time of need. This seed would yield great dividends in the future.

And when David heard that Nabal was dead, he said, Blessed be the LORD, that hath pleaded the cause of my reproach from the hand of Nabal, and hath kept his servant from evil: for the LORD hath returned the wickedness of Nabal upon his own head. And David sent and communed with Abigail, to take her to him to wife.

1 Samuel 25:39

Chapter 11

"He That Hath" Will Get Even More Because He Has Power to Get Wealth

Two Sources of Wealth

It takes power to get wealth. Wealth is not easy to come by. Anyone who has wealth has some kind of power working in his life that has drawn the wealth to him. Poor people do not have the power to get wealth. Some poor people seek for the power to get wealth in the wrong places. Through their desire for riches, they fall into all kinds of foolish and hurtful lusts which drown men in destruction and perdition.

"He that hath" money has been given power to get wealth. The power to get wealth comes from God. But it is not only God who gives the power to get wealth. The devil also gives people the power to get wealth. People are either anointed by God or anointed by the devil to get wealth.

Thus, there are two types of wealthy people in the world. One was given the power by God and the other was given the power by the devil. Let me share some Scriptures to prove that both God and the devil give people power to get wealth.

How Does the Devil Give Power to Get Wealth?

1. **The devil took Jesus to the mountain and showed Him the whole world and the glory of it and declared that it was his to give to whomever he wanted to.** From this Scripture you can see that the devil had the whole world and all its wealth in his hands. He offered it to Jesus Christ if He would only bow down. Jesus Christ refused to bow down and submit His ministry to the devil.

   The devil gives money to people who bow down to him. People submit their music, their films, their dances, their bodies and their talents to the devil. The devil uses their music and their talents for his purposes. Satan charges the masses with lust and perversions as the music of people who have sold their soul to the devil is played or sang.

   The devil gives money and wealth to politicians who submit their power to him. Many rulers of this world receive their power from evil spirits. That is why they lead nations into poverty, war and destruction. The rulers do not care about the people because they are inspired by demons who want to destroy God's creation.

   Again, the devil taketh him up into an exceeding high mountain, and sheweth him all the kingdoms of the world, and the glory of them;

   Matthew 4:8

2. **Wealth that the devil gives is wealth that comes with sorrow!** But the blessing of the Lord makes rich and adds no sorrow. There is a difference between the blessing of the Lord and other "blessings".

   The blessing of the Lord, it maketh rich, and he addeth no sorrow with it.
   Proverbs 10:22

   You may have some money and feel that God has blessed you. It is not only God who gives money to people. The devil can give people money.

   Have you noticed how many of the pop stars, film stars and soccer stars end up in sorrow and sadness?

   You wonder why the money was not able to make them happy.

   You wonder why they were not able to stay rich or maintain their apparent blessings.

   Indeed the blessing of the Lord maketh rich and he addeth no sorrow with it.

3. **Wealth that the devil gives is wealth that comes in the wrong way.** The Bible calls this getting wealth "not by right". This method of getting wealth is not something that God supports. Because God did not engineer this kind of wealth, He prophesies its doom.

   God declares that He will attack that wealth. The prophet declares that God will smite at your dishonest gain.

   As the partridge sitteth *on eggs*, and hatcheth *them* not; so HE THAT GETTETH RICHES, and NOT BY RIGHT, shall leave them in the midst of his days, and at his end shall be a fool.
   Jeremiah 17:11

"In you they have taken bribes to shed blood; you have taken interest and profits, and you have injured your neighbors for gain by oppression, and you have forgotten Me," declares the Lord GOD.

"Behold, then, I SMITE MY HAND AT YOUR DISHONEST GAIN which you have acquired and at the bloodshed which is among you."

Ezekiel 22:12-13 (NASB)

How Does God Make People Wealthy?

1.   God makes people wealthy by giving them *power* that specifically makes them wealthy.

But thou shalt remember the LORD thy God: for IT IS HE THAT GIVETH THEE POWER TO GET WEALTH, that he may establish his covenant which he sware unto thy fathers, as it is this day.

Deuteronomy 8:18

2.   God makes people wealthy by adding all things to their lives when they seek Him first.

But seek ye first the kingdom of God, and his righteousness; and all these things shall be added unto you.

Matthew 6:33

3.   God makes people wealthy by giving them *grace* that brings sufficiency.

There is a grace to have just enough. Having just enough

is what we call sufficiency. When the grace for sufficiency is on your life, you will have just enough all the time.

And GOD IS ABLE TO MAKE ALL GRACE ABOUND TOWARD YOU; that ye, always having all sufficiency in all things, may abound to every good work:

2 Corinthians 9:8

4. God makes people wealthy by breaking the curse of poverty.

There are curses that make people poor. Sometimes, poverty can only be explained by a curse. Sometimes, people have everything that should make them rich and prosperous. But somehow they never have enough. This should make you think of the possibility of a curse lurking around somewhere. The curse of the law included the law of poverty and Christ has redeemed us from that curse.

Christ hath REDEEMED US FROM THE CURSE OF THE LAW, being made a curse for us: for it is written, Cursed is every one that hangeth on a tree:

Galatians 3:13

5. God makes people wealthy by giving them the blessings of Abraham.

We are Abraham's children and the blessings of Abraham are coming on the Gentiles. We who are Gentiles are looking forward to the blessings of Abraham in our lives.

And Abram was very rich in cattle, in silver, and in gold.

Genesis 13:2

THAT THE BLESSING OF ABRAHAM MIGHT COME ON THE GENTILES through Jesus Christ; that we might receive the promise of the Spirit through faith.

Galatians 3:14

6. God makes people rich by giving them 'rain' which gives the increase to all they do.

ASK YE OF THE LORD RAIN in the time of the latter rain; so the LORD shall make bright clouds, and give them showers of rain, to every one grass in the field.

Zechariah 10:1

Be glad then, ye children of Zion, and rejoice in the LORD your God: for he hath given you the former rain moderately, and HE WILL CAUSE TO COME DOWN FOR YOU THE RAIN, the former rain, and the latter rain in the first month. And the floors shall be full of wheat, and the fats shall overflow with wine and oil.

Joel 2:23-24

7. God makes people rich by giving them the grace to give.

There are people who do not have the grace to give. When God wants to make you rich He will give you the ability to give. This is what the Bible calls "the grace for giving".

Therefore, as ye abound in every thing, in faith, and utterance, and knowledge, and in all diligence, and in your love to us, see that ye ABOUND IN THIS GRACE ALSO.

2 Corinthians 8:7

8. God makes people rich by giving them the spirit of wisdom.

The anointing for wealth releases the spirit of wisdom concerning wealth creation. Wisdom is what creates wealth. Wherever you find lasting wealth you find wise people. Praying for wisdom is like praying for wealth. Wisdom has a way of making you wealthy.

> Length of days is in her right hand; and in her left hand riches and honour.
>
> Proverbs 3:16

> Riches and honour are with me; yea, durable riches and righteousness.
>
> Proverbs 8:18

> Wisdom and knowledge is granted unto thee; and I will give thee riches, and wealth, and honour, such as none of the kings have had that have been before thee, neither shall there any after thee have the like.
>
> 2 Chronicles 1:12

9. God makes people wealthy by giving them particular talents and skills.

Many musicians, singers, soccer players, golf players, tennis players, basketball players, boxers and athletes were given talents by God to make them rich. Many of these people never glorified God or honoured him with their talents. The Scripture below shows that God is the source of wisdom, understanding and workmanship.

And I have filled him with the spirit of God, in wisdom, and in understanding, and in knowledge, and in all manner of workmanship,

Exodus 31:3

10. God makes people wealthy by making them diligent.

Diligence, relentless effort, is the greatest practical key to wealth creation. Without diligence all your theories will amount to nothing.

He becometh poor that dealeth with a slack hand: but the hand of the diligent maketh rich.

Proverbs 10:4

The thoughts of the diligent tend only to plenteousness; but of every one that is hasty only to want.

Proverbs 21:5

The soul of the sluggard desireth, and hath nothing: but the soul of the diligent shall be made fat.

Proverbs 13:4

Chapter 12

"He That Hath"
Will Get Even More Because
He Respects the Little
Difference That Makes
the Big Difference

Little things make a big difference. "He that hath" respects this reality that little things do make a big difference. At a certain level big things do not make a big difference. It is the little things that change everything. "He that hath" has learnt to respect little things and those little things have made a big difference in his life. Indeed, the difference between monkeys and human beings are very little things. It is amazing that little things can make the big difference that exists between monkeys and human beings. The Word of God is replete with examples of little things that make a big difference.

Ten Little Things That Make a Big Difference

1.   A little faith

...If ye have FAITH AS A GRAIN OF MUSTARD SEED, ye shall say unto this mountain, Remove hence to yonder place; and it shall remove; and nothing shall be impossible unto you.

Matthew 17:20

A little faith can make a big difference in your life.

Faith is important because you can only be saved through faith.

Faith is important because the elders received a good report through faith.

Faith is important because we live by faith.

Faith is important because we walk by faith.

Faith is important because without faith it is impossible to please God.

Amazingly, only a little faith is needed to accomplish great things with God. If you have faith as the smallest mustard seed you can move mountains.

2.   A little seed

And he said, whereunto shall we liken THE KINGDOM OF GOD? Or with what comparison shall we compare it?

IT IS LIKE A GRAIN OF MUSTARD SEED, which, when it is sown in the earth, is less than all the seeds that be in the earth: but when it is sown, it groweth up, and becometh greater than all herbs, and shooteth out great branches; so that the fowls of the air may lodge under the shadow of it.

Mark 4:30-32

The kingdom of God is also a small seed. This means that everything in the kingdom of God starts small but becomes great and mighty in the end. A church represents the kingdom of God, which starts out small and becomes a mighty tree.

A missionary who goes out into a country may seem insignificant. As the years go by, he will bear much fruit and become a mighty tree in the land. The Bible looks like an insignificant book in the hand of a preacher but that little book is a little seed that can change the lives of many people. Books, tapes, CDs, DVDs are little seeds that have a great impact.

3.   The little foxes

Take us the foxes, the little foxes, that spoil the vines: for our vines have tender grapes.

Song of Solomon 2:15

Little foxes speak of little things that can undermine great achievements.

The Little Phone

One day, I met a director of a large wealthy multi-national company. As I interacted with this executive I noticed his free use of his official phone and how other family members and friends could use his company phone to call anywhere in the world.

So I asked him how many directors and other staff members had such phones with such unlimited use. He explained that other directors and several other staff below his rank had such phones and they all had unlimited use of the phone.

He then offered the phone to me and asked if I needed to call anywhere in the world. Indeed, I enjoyed several hours of free long-distance international calls. That day I predicted the collapse of this multi-national company and I was not wrong. A few years later, the entire company collapsed from within. Perhaps, the little phone with its bills was making a big difference.

The Little Bulb

One day, I visited my grandfather and grandmother in Switzerland. I had a nice time. But one day, my grandfather got angry with me, waved his walking stick at me and shouted at me in German. I wondered what terrible crime I had committed. I was surprised to find out that I had left a few bulbs on. What could be so wrong with leaving some lights on in the corridor? Why was he angry about something so little?

As I grew up, I found out that this "little thing" of wasting electricity was a characteristic of poor people. Developing countries without much money leave lights on and waste electricity all the time, whilst the rich tend to save electricity.

Leaving lights on and wasting electricity undermines all your efforts to save money and become rich.

4.   A little leaven

A little leaven leaveneth the whole lump.

Galatians 5:9

A little leaven can affect everything. This Scripture speaks of the influence that a little error can have. A little error in the doctrines of the leader can lead to the destruction of many lives. Entire churches and denominations are led into lukewarmness and fruitlessness because of a little difference in doctrine. The church's failure to teach about salvation through faith and grace, created a totally backslidden church whose members bought their salvation with money.

Some Bibles say that Jesus Christ was born of a young woman. They do not state that Jesus Christ was born of a virgin. Although there seems to be just a little difference between a young woman and a virgin, it makes a huge difference to who Jesus Christ was. If He was born of a virgin then He was supernatural and had fulfilled an ancient prophecy (Isaiah 7:14). If He was just born of a young woman then He was just like any of us.

Failing to talk about miracles and healing creates a powerless church that is very different from the church Christ left. Indeed, there are many things to preach about without touching on the subject of the anointing or the healing power of God. "Having a form of godliness, but denying the power thereof: from such turn away" (2 Timothy 3:5).

Failing to talk about Heaven and eternity can make a big difference in the type of congregation we see. The modern church conveniently shies away from the discussion of Hell. This makes a huge difference and has created a powerless church whose heart is set on earthly things.

5.   Little books

And the voice which I heard from heaven spake unto me again, and said, Go and take the little book which is open in the hand of the angel which standeth upon the sea and upon the earth.

And I went unto the angel, and said unto him, give me THE LITTLE BOOK. And he said unto me, Take it, and eat it up; and it shall make thy belly bitter, but it shall be in thy mouth sweet as honey.

And I took THE LITTLE BOOK out of the angel's hand, and ate it up; and it was in my mouth sweet as honey: and as soon as I had eaten it, my belly was bitter.

And he said unto me, Thou must prophesy again before many peoples, and nations, and tongues, and kings.

Revelation 10:8-11

The revelation found in a little book can make a difference for your ministry. Many years ago I was introduced to a little book by Kenneth Hagin. This little book introduced me to the person who was to teach me about faith and about the ministry. Without going to Bible school and without having the support of certain ministers of the gospel, a little book raised me out of nowhere to write this book to you. You are reading this book today because of the power of little books.

6.   Little children

But Jesus said, Suffer little children, and forbid them not, to come unto me: for of such is the kingdom of heaven.

Matthew 19:14

Little children are often discounted as being insignificant. Yet, it is the little children who are the key to the expansion of the kingdom. Little children are the key to your church growth. Little children are the key to your missionary work. Little children are the people who will respond to you and to your evangelistic efforts. Jesus said that the kingdom of Heaven is made up of such people.

Little children are also the key to greatness because Jesus taught that the humility of children was the greatest key to greatness. Jesus said the greatest person was the little child. A child's ability to forgive and forget is a revelation of true greatness. A child's ability to play with other children of other backgrounds is a revelation of true greatness. A child's ability to learn and copy is a revelation of true greatness. A child's ability to copy from another is a revelation of true greatness.

Indeed, little children although little can make a great difference in our lives if we will learn from them and become like them.

7. The little member of the body

Even so the tongue is a little member, and boasteth great things. Behold, how great a matter a little fire kindleth!

And the tongue *is* a fire, a world of iniquity: so is the tongue among our members, that it defileth the whole body, and setteth on fire the course of nature; and it is set on fire of hell.

James 3:5-6

The tongue is a little part of the whole body and yet it can control everything that happens in your life. Death and life are in the power of the tongue... (Proverbs 18:21). Whosoever will say to a mountain be thou removed into the sea and does not doubt will have what he says. There seems to be much power in what you say with your tongue. All through the Bible, the power of the tongue is emphasized. You are snared by the words of your mouth. Although a little thing, it can make a big difference.

8.   A little wine

Drink no longer water, but use A LITTLE WINE for thy stomach's sake and thine often infirmities.

1 Timothy 5:23

A little wine could make a big difference to Timothy's health. How important it is to believe that little things can make a big difference to our health. Little sips of Coca Cola could make a big difference to your size and weight. Little tablets taken everyday could make a big difference to how long you live. Lazy people do not care about these little things which will make a big difference. They eat anything and drink anything because they assume that a little thing cannot make a big difference.

9.   A little slumber

Yet a little sleep, a little slumber, a little folding of the hands to sleep:

So shall thy poverty come *as* one that travelleth; and thy want as an armed man.

Proverbs 24:33-34

A little more sleep can make a big difference to your financial situation. A little sleep, when you should have been studying can mean that you become a clerk instead of a lawyer. A little sleep, when you should have been studying could mean that you become a nurse rather than a doctor.

A little sleep instead of working hard on your campaign could mean that you will lose an election. A little sleep instead of diligently working on your farm could mean that your chickens could be eaten by a fox. It may be an hour's sleep or a few minutes rest, but you must be careful. Resting and relaxing too early can be a most dangerous activity.

10.   A little folly

Dead flies cause the ointment of the apothecary to send forth a stinking savour: so *doth* a little folly him that is in reputation for wisdom and honour.

Ecclesiastes 10:1

A little folly is a little foolishness. Great honour can be destroyed with a little foolishness. Many mighty men have learnt that a little folly is enough to destroy a lifetime of honourable works. It is important to pray to the Lord for deliverance from the snares and the traps of foolishness that lurk in the shadows of the paths of all great men.

Chapter 13

How a Little Difference between Apes and Men Makes a Big Difference

For years, it has been known that there are many similarities between apes and human beings. Monkeys are the animals that most closely resemble human beings. But what is the difference between monkeys and human beings? Are there big differences between human beings and monkeys? The answer is no.

There are very little differences between apes and human beings. Surprisingly, it is these little differences that make the big difference between monkeys and human beings. It is these little differences that have allowed human beings to develop into a civilization that dominates the world. Human beings have developed sophisticated cars, aeroplanes, and all sorts of gadgets like televisions, radios, phones and computers. Human beings have come together in groups and formed nations that have conquered other nations. Human beings have explored the planet earth and visited the moon.

Why Have Monkeys Not Become a Great Race?

But why have monkeys not been able to organize themselves into nations?

Why have monkeys not invented anything?

Why have monkeys not developed a language, a currency or the art of writing and reading?

Why don't they have great libraries where they can record their history? Is there a big difference between apes and human beings?

The answer is no. There is not a big difference between monkeys and human beings. There is very little difference. But it is that little difference that makes the big difference!

Why have they not taken over the world from human beings as is shown in some movies.

Why have they not come out of the forest and invaded the known civilizations of the world.

Why do they remain in the forest at the mercy of leopards, hyenas and other predators? Why don't apes develop clothes, shoes and perfumes?

Why don't apes have shops and houses?

Why are they not able to do these great things that human beings have done? Is it a "big" difference that is making such a "big" difference between monkeys and human beings? *What is holding the monkeys back?* The answer is very simple. It is a little difference that is holding the monkeys back.

The Rich and the Poor

Similarly, the differences between the rich and the poor are not caused by big things. The big things are usually the same. All human beings have similarly sized and similarly equipped brains, hearts, kidneys, lungs, etc. These are the big organs in a human being. No one can create them or change them. But there are little differences between human beings that create a class of rich people and a class of poor people.

Amazingly, it is these little differences that make the big differences between rich countries and poor countries.

If you are striving for greatness in the ministry or in the financial world, always remember that it is little things that separate the rich from the poor. It is little things that separate the successful from the failures.

In this short section, I want you to notice how similar apes and human beings are. On the other hand, I want you to notice the little differences that exist between apes and human beings.

Twelve Similarities between Apes and Human Beings

1.   Apes and humans live and move in groups.

2.   Apes and humans are both territorial and tend to be aggressive in the defence of their territories.

3.   Apes and humans usually resolve conflict through various submissive and appeasement behaviours.

Conflict within ape and human groups frequently develops out of competition for resources, including mating partners and food items.

4. Apes and humans both make sounds in communicating.

5. Apes like humans use a range of non-verbal communicative social skills such as facial expressions, eye gaze and manual gestures.

6. Ape and human societies are usually dominated by the male species.

7. Both apes and humans share common behaviours that involve various forms of physical contact including touching, hand holding, hugging, and, among chimpanzees, kissing.

8. Both apes and humans share a mother-infant bond. This bond is usually the strongest and most lasting bond. It may last for many years; commonly for the lifetime of the mother.

9. Both apes and humans are similar in their style of play. They both use their playtime as a means of learning. For example, Chimpanzee infants mimic the food-getting activities of their mothers, "attack" dozing adults, and "harass" adolescents.

10. Both ape and human groups and societies are organized based on similar factors. E.g. rank, status etc. Individual rank or status may be measured by access to resources, including food items and mating partners.

11. The way humans elect their political leaders mirrors the way an alpha male gains power. Chimpanzee

dominance is not determined by strength or size. Rather, a highly organized coalition of animals must support, or elect, their leader.

12. Both humans and apes react to unfair treatment. The renowned Yerkes primatologist designed an experiment in which two side-by-side apes were rewarded with the same food after completing the same task. Both animals repeated the task to continue to receive the reward. When one of the apes began to be rewarded for the same task with a better treat, the other animal, observing the unfair treatment, quickly refused to repeat the task, effectively going on strike.

Eight Little Differences between Monkeys and Human Beings That Make the Big Difference

1. Apes can copy just like human children copy their parents. But there is a little difference between the copying of an ape and the copying of a human. **CHILDREN COPY MORE MINDLESSLY AND MORE COMPLETELY BECAUSE THEY VIEW THE PERSON AS A TEACHER OR A GROWN-UP WHO KNOWS SOMETHING IMPORTANT.**

The ape's ability to copy is flawed. The ape copies in an incomplete way. This minor difference in the way apes copy leads to a major difference in the outcome of the lives of monkeys and humans.

Similarly, there is a big difference between human beings who copy mindlessly and completely and those who don't. Human beings who copy other humans completely have a higher quality of life and a superior civilization.

For instance, European countries are almost identical in their economies, infrastructure and wealth. If you drove through France, Italy, Switzerland and Germany you wouldn't easily be able to tell the differences between them. These countries became equally wealthy by emulating each other. In recent times, countries like Korea and China which have mindlessly and completely copied developed countries have advanced significantly to the amazement of the rest of the world. It is the little difference in *their ability to copy completely and totally* that makes a big difference between them and other darker underdeveloped sections of the world.

In your ministry, *your ability to copy completely and totally will always set you miles apart from other ministers* who are unable to completely copy what they see in other great ministers of the Gospel.

Copying is the most advanced form of learning. It is the natural ability given to every child who comes into this world. Copying has gotten a bad name because some people have copied in examinations. But this is not what I am talking about. I am talking about the ability to learn and improve by wholeheartedly and absolutely copying a successful person.

Copying completely is important because there are many things successful ministries do that they do not talk about. Many successful people do not know what makes them successful. If you were to ask them what their secrets of success were they would probably tell you a very small part of what has made them successful. That is why you must learn from what people say as well as what they do.

This is why the Bible records both the teachings and the lives of people. God ministers to us through their lives as well as through their teachings. Even Jesus did not teach all His principles of success. This is why Luke recorded both what Jesus did and what He said. Notice: "The former treatise have I made, O Theophilus, of *all that Jesus began both to do and teach*, Until the day in which he was taken up, after that he through the Holy Ghost had given commandments unto the apostles whom he had chosen" (Acts 1:1-2).

2. Apes learn from their parents as do human beings. Apes are taught by their parents just as children are taught by their parents. But there is *a little difference* between the teaching of an ape and the learning of a human. **APES DO NOT GATHER THEIR CHILDREN INTO GROUPS TO TEACH THEM WHAT THEY KNOW.**

Apes cannot sit down in a classroom to be taught important things in a systematic way. This little difference makes a big difference. The civilizations and developments of human beings far outstrip the civilization and development of apes because of this little difference.

Similarly, churches or organizations which cannot make groups sit down to be taught important things are completely different from those who are able to gather the congregation into groups and teach them systematically for many hours.

3. In the processes of learning, there are little differences that constantly magnify the differences between apes and human beings. One such little difference is **THE ABILITY TO POINT AT IMPORTANT THINGS AND UNDERSTAND WHAT IS BEING POINTED AT.** Pointing shows what my attention is on and what I want your attention to be on. A mother is constantly trying

to show things to the child. Pointing silently is giving direction, guidance and teaching.

A little difference between a child and a monkey is that the human child begins to point at things and to notice things that are pointed to. **AMAZINGLY APES ARE CLUELESS WHEN THINGS ARE POINTED TO OR AT.** If your attention cannot be drawn to an important thing, how can you develop properly?

Similarly, differences between human beings become more obvious when their attention cannot be drawn to the important things. A boss points out to his employees the important things that need to be done. He points out why it must be done by a certain time. And yet many employees do not get it. No matter how many hours he points to the key and critical issues, they do not seem to do what he says. Surely, these are employees who will not be promoted. This causes employees to remain in darkness.

In certain countries fingers are pointed to the absence of democracy and bad leadership. But somehow, the nation does not seem to get it. All they want is loans and gifts from richer nations. At other times, fingers will point at the absence of industries and the absence of rich people in the country. Yet the people in power are unable to see what is being pointed at.

Because of this inability to see what is being pointed at, huge differences emerge between different groups of people. Extremely poor groups of people live in a world which has extremely rich people. Yet we wonder what is making the big differences between groups of people on the same planet. *Things are being pointed out and yet groups of people are unable to understand what is being pointed at.* The huge differences between human beings are caused by failing to work on things that are pointed at!

4. Both apes and human beings can understand words and obey instructions. You will see monkeys in circuses and zoos performing little tricks to impress their audiences. Obviously, apes can understand words and obey some instructions. However, there is a little difference between the communication of human beings and the communication of apes. **APES CANNOT ENGAGE IN A CONVERSATION. THEY CANNOT RESPOND TO LITTLE COMMENTS. THEY CANNOT ASK QUESTIONS. THEY CANNOT SEEK CLARI-FICATION.** This little difference causes the colossal difference between the lives of monkeys and the lives of human beings.

Similarly, human beings who do not ask questions, make comments or seek clarification on issues grow up to become completely different from those who do.

Some groups of human beings live from generation to generation without asking, "Who lives behind that mountain? Is there anything beyond those peaks?" They never ask questions about what lies on the other side of the sea. But there are other groups of people on earth who ask the question, "Is the earth flat or round? Is there anyone beyond the horizon? Is there land? Are there people? Is there water beyond what my eye can see?"

ASKING QUESTIONS AND SEEKING CLARI-FICATION MAY SEEM LIKE A LITTLE THING. BUT IT IS THAT WHICH HAS MADE A DIFFERENCE BETWEEN DIFFERENT GROUPS OF PEOPLE ON EARTH. People have searched for big differences to explain the disparity between groups of people. They have tried to measure brain size, intelligence and IQ. They always came up with a blank because the big things are the same.

God made us all the same and equally capable. It is little differences that make the big difference. Today, some people want to know whether there is water and life on Mars whilst others cannot find water on earth to flush their toilets. Have you noticed how some groups on the planet seek to study and to understand lions, leopards, antelopes, worms, flies, birds, sharks, whales and snakes? Other groups of people just kill them when they come across them. These little differences cause the disparity that you see in people.

In the ministry, the large differences between ministers and churches is also caused by this very thing. Some people never ask, "Why is this person able to have a big church? How were you able to do this? Is it the anointing? If it is the anointing how can I also have the anointing? How did you get that anointing?" Sadly, many ministers do not seek clarification. Many ministers do not ask questions. They just assume that they know. They just assume that there are negative reasons for people's success. Because of this, big differences develop between ministers with the same kind of divine call.

5. Apes lack the ability to cheer others on which is a basic teacher's skill. **THIS INABILITY TO CHEER AND ENCOURAGE OTHERS ON AFFECTS THEIR ABILITY TO RECOGNIZE GREATNESS. BECAUSE THEY DO NOT RECOGNIZE GREAT-NESS THEY HAVE NO ONE TO EMULATE.** Inability of monkeys to cheer each other and encourage

others also inhibits their ability to teach each other. This little thing which is absent in the teaching practices of monkeys causes the great difference between a monkey and a human being. It is what makes *us* catch *them* and put *them* into cages and observe *them* instead of *them* catching *us* and putting *us* behind prison bars.

Both apes and human beings have things to teach their young. Even lions have been observed teaching their young how to hunt and how to kill. But because of these little differences in teaching between monkeys and human beings vital information is not passed on to the next generation of monkeys.

A lack of teaching locks in or freezes the progress a generation has made in any sphere of life. Among monkeys, there is a loss of the achievements and cultural innovations made by a generation. Humans have both the passion and mental skills to teach each other.

Perhaps this is why Solomon kept hammering, "My son attend to the words of thy father." He wanted to pass on the progress, the knowledge, the achievements and the skills acquired by the father. Each generation invents a simple thing. The next generation learns the simple version but then adds on some complexity to it. That is what has created the advanced culture of humans. The absence of this little ability to pass knowledge to the next generation is what creates the big difference between monkeys and human beings.

There is a big difference between people who learn from history. People who learn from fathers are blessed. People who despise fathers and forerunners cut their own lives short.

They are doomed to a far lower quality of life because they would not receive the knowledge and experiences of the fathers. Human beings who respect history, study biographies and learn from the past are vastly different from those who march on as champions of ignorance.

6. Apes lack the ability to cooperate. They do cooperate in a very limited way. Their lack of cooperation is what prevents them from planning an attack on human civilizations. They are unable to have meetings in the jungle to decide on a plan of action. They are unable to meet to strategize on how to collectively outwit their human hunters. **THIS INABILITY TO COOPERATE IS THE LITTLE DIFFERENCE THAT MAKES AN IMMENSE DIFFERENCE BETWEEN THE LIVES OF APES AND HUMAN BEINGS.**

The inability to choose a leader, to assist a leader and to work together for a common goal is what keeps the monkeys in the forest whilst you and I dwell happily ever after in the cities.

This inability to cooperate is the little difference that makes the big difference between nations. *The inability to choose a leader democratically, the inability to agree that it will be your turn for four years and after that it will be my turn causes colossal differences between the nations on our planet.* In some countries, the cooperation is so high that the president is not even elected but simply rotated from one region to another.

The ability to cooperate is what creates companies, banks, stock exchanges, mergers and multinational concerns. The ability to cooperate is what creates football clubs which become multimillion dollar enterprises and provide jobs for millions. The inability to cooperate fails to understand that, after you have eaten, I will also eat; after you have benefitted I will also benefit. This is the difference that causes the sad disparity between groups of people. You will notice that the more human beings have these characteristics the darker and less developed their lives become.

The ability to collectively build a church, supporting and cooperating with the leadership is vital for us to move away from the darkness of the forest and jungle life.

7. Monkeys can recognize the ascending nature of numbers but cannot put them together and subtract. **MONKEYS CANNOT ADD, WHICH MEANS THEY CANNOT COMPREHEND HOW THIS AND THIS LEAD TO THAT.** It is this inability to put complex things together and see how one unrelated thing leads to another that sets the brain of a monkey apart from the brain of a human being.

In the human world, however, this principle works to separate the rich from the poor. Surprisingly, poor countries specialize in the very things that generate poverty. Poor countries continue to specialize in the very activities that only spell more poverty. Perhaps, this is because the correlation between certain activities and poverty is not easy to see. Most of the great achievements of mankind have come about through the development of complicated or complex things.

Rich nations seem to know how "this and this leads to that". They have therefore emphasized on certain things which have always generated wealth. Rich countries emphasize on what is called "increasing returns activities (industries) and imperfect markets (selling cars, computers, phones whose prices are subjectively and imperfectly determined by the makers of these things). Rich countries emphasize on innovations and technological change." These words sound complicated and they are indeed. But it is complex factors that generate riches.

Sadly, poor countries do not seem to see how "this and this leads to that". They therefore emphasize on diminishing return activities (farming, mining, and fishing) and perfect markets (selling things like gold, coffee, tea and bananas whose prices are perfectly determined by the world market). Poor countries emphasize on activities like farming which have little innovation and little technological change. All these complicated-sounding things are the causes of poverty. A failure to add two and two together is a cause of deepening poverty in the already poor sections of the world.

8. Both monkeys and human beings have greedy urges and emotions.

But there is a little difference between the emotions and urges of monkeys and humans. **MONKEYS NEVER OVERCOME OR CONTROL THEIR GREEDY URGES. A MONKEY'S RESPONSE TO A BANANA WILL NEVER CHANGE.** It will always be the same and it will never vary. Human beings are much less impulsive in their reactions and impulses.

The response of a human being to food will vary according to what he thinks it should be. Monkeys never think it should be different. When impulse control was tested on different children *it was found that the longer a child resisted his urges and impulses, the higher his academic performance was in later years.*

It is a reality that we all have impulses and urges. The little difference is in the ability to control these urges. In some countries or churches, the leaders are unable to control their urge to take all the money and hide it away for themselves. This inability to control the urge to take as much as possible creates the difference between rich countries or churches and the poorer countries or churches.

The leaders of poor countries have been known to stash away millions of dollars which they can never use. They mindlessly stash away huge sums of money because they cannot control the urge to take more and more. Amazingly, this little difference creates the massive differences we see in the world today.

Chapter 14

"He That Hath"
Does Not Waste the Good
Things That Come from God

Why People Who Waste Things Become Poor

1. **Waste provokes the start of a bad season of difficulty, frustration and poverty.**

    And he said also unto his disciples, There was a certain rich man, which had a steward; and the same was accused unto him that HE HAD WASTED HIS GOODS.

    Luke 16:1

    ecause the steward wasted his master's goods he was
    about to lose his job and begin a new season of want
    and difficulty in his life. He had provoked the

beginning of a bad season because of his wasteful way of working. Wasting good things has a way of provoking bad and difficult seasons in our lives.

This rich man had certain goods that were in the charge of the steward. In the same way, God has given us everything we have in this life. You are the custodian of God's resources and God expects you not to waste them.

Whoever you are, know that God has placed certain things in your charge. He has put your life in your hands; He has given you parents, children, lands, trees, rivers, money and opportunities. But God's expectation is that you use them wisely. If you waste the blessings and opportunities that God puts in your hands, do not be surprised at the bad seasons of difficulty, stress, frustrations and want that descend upon you.

2.   Waste causes you to lose your position and this brings you into poverty.

And he said also unto his disciples, There was a certain rich man, which had a steward; and the same was accused unto him that he had WASTED his goods.

And he called him, and said unto him, How is it that I hear this of thee? give an account of thy stewardship; FOR THOU MAYEST BE NO LONGER STEWARD.

Luke 16:1-2

If you waste what God has put into your hand you will lose your valued and privileged position. If you don't use the resources wisely, you will end up poor. Just as this prodigal steward was asked to account for his stewardship, God will ask you to account for yours. I believe that many Christians are failing because they are wasting the resources God has given them. God may not remind you of the education He gave you, the job He gave you, or the life He gave you. God will give to you over and over again, but one day, He will ask you to give an account of what is in your control. If you can't account properly for these things you will lose your position.

3. **Wasters are often deceived about how wealth is created and therefore destroy wealth by their lifestyles.**

Wasters tend to become poor whilst those who can bring a halt to the wastage tend to become rich.

And the younger of them said to *his* father, Father, give me the portion of goods that falleth *to me*. And he divided unto them *his* living.

And not many days after the younger son gathered all together, and took his journey into a far country, and there WASTED HIS SUBSTANCE with riotous living.

And when he had spent all, there arose a mighty famine in that land; and he began to be in want.

Luke 15:12-14

When you can stop the things that waste away your money, you will become rich. In the Bible, the things that waste your money are called devourers. Few people realise the correlation between the devourer and the creation of real wealth. People are more prosperous when they live in places with fewer devourers.

Unfortunately, places with fewer devourers are often unattractive to live in but those who have had the boldness to live in places like that usually enjoy a much higher quality of life. Africa and other poorer developing countries have fewer "established devourers."

> Bring ye all the tithes into the storehouse, that there may be meat in mine house, and prove me now herewith, saith the LORD of hosts, if I will not open you the windows of heaven, and pour you out a blessing, that *there shall not be room enough to receive it.*
>
> And I will rebuke the devourer for your sakes, and he shall not destroy the fruits of your ground; neither shall your vine cast her fruit before the time in the field, saith the LORD of hosts.
>
> Malachi 3:10-11

God's promise to tithers is to rebuke the devourer. God did not promise to increase the income of tithers. He promised to rebuke the devourer or the waster. The creation of wealth is not dependent on how much you earn but on how much gets wasted.

Many people earn a lot but pay out a lot more. This is why people with high salaries often do not have much money to spend. The devourer takes away everything. Well-known and "established devourers" include things like the rent, the mortgage, the car bills, the water bills, the heating bills, the electricity bills, the gas bills, the property rates, poll tax, income tax, gift tax, waste management bills, staff salaries, health bills, insurance bills, shopping bills, groceries bills, parking bills, traffic over-speeding fines, holidays, new cars, etc., until there is nothing left.

4.   Wasters become poor because they are brothers of lazy people.

He also that is slothful in his work is BROTHER TO HIM THAT IS A GREAT WASTER.

Proverbs 18:9

Years ago, my father owned a hotel and it seemed that it was not doing well. He hired a professional hotel manager to run it but the profits were still not coming in. Unknown to him, all his profits were leaking out through the nefarious activities of the hotel staff. Indeed, a waster is a brother to a lazy person. In other words, they are from the same family and therefore give the same effect.

One day, something happened and he sacked most of the staff including the manager. He then asked me if I knew anyone who could run a hotel. I said I did not know any hotel manager but I had a close friend who was honest. He asked me to bring this friend along and he hired him instantly. This friend of mine had no idea about managing a hotel but he was an honest person.

Can you believe that the income of the hotel jumped from fifteen units to about a thousand units overnight? My friend had not introduced any new hotel management ideas into the business. He just did not steal and waste as the last group had been doing.

Suddenly, with the devourer rebuked, the income of this hotel skyrocketed. To me, that was one of the greatest lessons on the importance of rebuking the devourer. It is not about how much is coming in. It is all about how well you can paralyse the devourers around you.

Years ago, I walked through some shops in Europe with a friend of mine who was, unknown to me, a petty thief. To my utter surprise, when we came out of the shop she showed me the things she had stolen. I could not believe my eyes but she was excited about her booty.

She told me that it was something she did all the time. Then I realised that there were many people like that who constantly stole from large shops and supermarkets. It is no wonder that many people who have large shops and supermarkets rarely make profits. The devourers walk through the shops and take away all the profit.

After this event, I noticed a trend in which shops began to invest in CCTV and other modern forms of security. Through various innovative and hi-tech measures, many large shops and supermarkets have fought the stealing menace and become profitable again.

Indeed, the profitability of these shops simply depended on fighting the devourer. This is the very thing that God promises to do when you pay your tithes. Tithe paying invokes the significant blessing of having the devourer and waster rebuked.

Once the devourer is rebuked in your life, once the waste in your life is stopped, your wealth and assets will begin to increase. This is why people who pay tithes can become rich – the devourers in their lives are rebuked by the Lord.

5. **Wasters are destroyers of wealth because they do not know or understand what valuable things are.**

Behold, I have created the smith that bloweth the coals in the fire, and that bringeth forth an

instrument for his work; AND I HAVE CREATED THE WASTER TO DESTROY.

Isaiah 54:16

A waster usually becomes a destroyer because he does not appreciate valuable things. He does not even know what he is handling. Truly valuable things are determined by what the Bible says, and not what you think. God is wiser than us. God knows more than we do and He will show us what is truly valuable. The Word of God is our reliable guide as to what is truly valuable. The Word of God gives life, light and direction as to what is valuable. God expects us to seek His will concerning what is valuable.

In a remote diamond mining African village, children would play with what they thought were ordinary stones. One day, someone came along and informed them that the stones they were throwing at each other were actually diamonds. They stopped throwing the "stones" at each other and began to treat them with the respect they deserved. They had realized that these "stones" would bring them great wealth. Your life will change when you discover how important something is.

It is very important to esteem, treasure and *place value* on things in your life. All over the world, people attend school just to learn how to value properties. These are professionals called "valuers" or "land economists".

When you know the value of something you will not misuse it. There are some things that you do not regard because you do not know their importance. Many people only value money! But it is important to know that apart from money, many other things are valuable. Sometimes people go to great lengths to explain how expensive something is. This is because they want you to recognize how valuable what they have given you is.

I once bought a present for a couple. When I gave it to them, they looked at it almost with disdain. I knew immediately that they didn't know how much it cost. So I told them how much their present cost me. I saw an immediate change in their countenance. They got up and moved towards the gift to have a closer look at it.

Sometimes it is important to explain the value of things to people so that they treat it well.

Twelve Things That Rich People Do Not Waste

1.   "He that hath" does not waste the crumbs of his life.

Jesus taught a great lesson when He gathered the crumbs after feeding the multitude on the mountain. During one of Jesus' evangelistic tours, there were more than five thousand people He needed to feed. Philip, one of Jesus' disciples pointed out that even two hundred penny worth of bread would not be sufficient to feed them.

But a small boy's lunch of five barley loaves of bread and two small fish was blessed by Jesus, and He fed them all.

When they were filled, he said unto his disciples, Gather up the fragments that remain, that nothing be lost.

John 6:12

Instead of just sharing the grace and leaving, He collected twelve baskets of crumbs. I am sure every one of His twelve disciples took a basket home!

If you want to follow somebody, follow Jesus. He is the express image of God Himself. To see what God Himself would have done, look at Jesus - He gathered the crumbs after He had taken five thousand people to the restaurant. Why would someone who could afford to take five thousand people to the restaurant be interested in crumbs? The answer is simple: Avoiding waste! Frugality! Fighting waste!

I can say from my little experience in this life, that it is often rich people who gather crumbs. **If you do not come to the place where crumbs are important to you, you will never be rich, neither will you prosper.**

The Lord told me when we started our church building project, "If you count your pennies, you will always have enough."

I have found God's words to be true. In our church we don't have any big business tycoon who pays for massive sections of our projects. Most people are just average. Yet, we have gone very far and completed projects worth millions of dollars. We gathered the crumbs! Crumbs are important to us.

Most people in poor developing countries do not respect the crumbs. Lights which are not in use are left switched on and water is left dripping from the taps. Water leaks from the pipes all the time and no one is bothered.

When I visited my grandparents in Switzerland, I realized the waste in Africa. I would leave my lights on all the time. In Switzerland, only the rooms in which we were present had lights on. Every other room was in darkness to save electricity.

My grandfather would come with his walking stick and say, "You! You!"

Then he would shake his stick, and I would know that he wanted me to turn off the extra lights.

Sometimes you wonder why certain people prosper and some do not. Switzerland is one of the richest countries in the world. In 1993, the GDP of Switzerland was 219 billion dollars while that of Ghana was only about 6 billion dollars

In poor Ghana, we waste electricity and become poorer. In rich Switzerland, they save electricity and become richer!

It is the crumbs that make up the whole meal. When you save up all your crumbs, you will become rich.

There's a saying that "little drops of water make a mighty ocean". That's not in the Bible, but it's true.

The population of the world has been on a steady rise since 1900. Before the turn of the twentieth century, the world's population had been steady at about the same figure for many years. Suddenly the population of the world began to rise dramatically.

What happened to make the number of people in the world increase?

It was largely due to the great advances in medicine. There are now cures for most of the killer diseases that wiped out huge numbers of people. When the death rate went down, the number of people went up. If you reduce the amount of deaths (dropouts or waste) your wealth will rise.

If you can stay at the same income level and reduce the waste, you will increase and become rich.

Pastors need to learn that if they can only reduce the number of people dropping out of their churches, the churches will grow.

I value every single member of my church. I try hard to prevent people leaving the church.

I want to close the back door of the church. Many churches have big front doors and big back doors; that's why they never grow!

Your business will grow when you can stop the waste and prevent high, unnecessary bills. Don't you realize that all your profits and increase are going down the drain?

Monitor your electricity bills, water bills and telephone bills on a chart. All these bills are draining you of your increase.

2. "He that hath" does not waste the good fathers and mothers that God has given him. He that hath not is a waster of the good fathers given to him by God.

Honour thy father and mother; (which is the first commandment with promise;)

Ephesians 6:2

It will do you a world of good to value the fathers and mothers God has provided for you. The absence of a father or a mother has untold effects on children. Unfortunately, mothers and fathers are often valued only after they are dead.

I once noticed a man carrying a huge wreath on board a flight from Amsterdam to Accra. It was the most beautiful set of flowers I had ever seen. It was so big that he had to put it on one of the empty seats and buckle it up with a seat belt. He was apparently on his way to bury his mother. I wondered if he had bought such flowers for her when she was alive. I also wondered if he had visited her when she was alive.

We must place value on people and things while we have them with us, or we will live to regret it. The principle of valuation teaches us to value what we have, so that we treat it with care, so we can benefit from it.

3.   "He that hath" does not waste a good wife God has given him. He that hath not is a waster of the good wife given to him by God.

Who can find a virtuous woman? for her price is far above rubies.

Proverbs 31:10

Many unsuccessful men have wives behind the scenes who fight and oppose them. The presence of an evil woman in a man's life can be so devastating. It is when you see a non-virtuous woman in action that you understand the value of a virtuous woman. The virtuous woman is really very valuable because there are not many genuinely virtuous women. Remember that a high demand with a low supply is what raises the prices of anything. The low supply of virtuous women is what has raised her price above rubies.

4.   "He that hath" does not waste a good name. He that hath not is a waster of good names.

A good name is rather to be chosen than great riches, and loving favour rather than silver and gold.

Proverbs 22:1

A good name is better than precious ointment; and the day of death than the day of one's birth.

Ecclesiastes 7:1

You may not know how valuable a good name is. There are some places I have been to where I have had (as it were) a "good" name, and others where I have a "bad" name. It often depends on whether my enemies or friends have been there before me and what they have said about me! Through experience I have found that a good name is better than riches. You cannot flourish in the atmosphere created by a bad name. You cannot buy a good name with money. I have learnt to value a good name. You will too! Once a reputation of a school is lowered, it is difficult to build it up again. A good name is indeed better than riches.

5. **"He that hath" does not waste the humble things God brings to him. He that hath not is a waster and despiser of the humble things of his life.**

By faith Moses, when he was come to years, refused to be called the son of Pharaoh's daughter; Choosing rather to suffer affliction with the people of God, than to enjoy the pleasures of sin for a season; ESTEEMING THE REPROACH OF CHRIST GREATER RICHES than the treasures in Egypt: for he had respect unto the recompence of the reward.

Hebrews 11:24-26

Moses knew the value of the reproach that he was experiencing. It would work out in him a greater blessing than all the riches of Egypt.

Paul knew the value of the trials, reproaches and distressing situations he was experiencing in this life. He could see through it and beyond it. He knew that there was a great blessing hidden in the very thing that people despised him for.

> And He has said to me, "My grace is sufficient for you, for power is perfected in weakness." Most gladly, therefore, I will rather boast about my weaknesses, that the power of Christ may dwell in me."
>
> Therefore I am well content with weaknesses, with insults, with distresses, with persecutions, with difficulties, for Christ's sake; for when I am weak, then I am strong.
>
> 2 Corinthians 12:9, 10 (NASB)

Unfortunately, those whose minds do not have the latitude to comprehend the good that will come out of certain things are continually discontent and fail to receive God's blessings through the humble things of their lives. They go out chasing fantasies and things that will not profit them. Instead of being content with what God has given them, they are constantly out and about following things which yield very little fruit.

People Who Despise Humble Things
Love to Chase Fantasies

There is a verse that tells us that if a man has a humble piece of land right before him, and makes use of it, he will have more than enough food to eat. But if this man rather chases after what he imagines he can get from somewhere else, then he will be poor forever!

He who works his land will have abundant food, but the one who chases fantasies will have his fill of poverty.

Proverbs 28:19 (NIV)

For this man, the difference between abundance and poverty will be determined by whether he works on the piece of land he has, or whether he runs after fantasies and unreal goals.

The piece of land here could be his humble profession, job, or property. He may own a shop or restaurant. He may be a teacher, doctor, or a photographer. Whatever the profession, he must make good use of it.

Unfortunately, many people waste their lives chasing fantasies. Fantasies are things that are not real; they are things that are not in your hands. If you have a bird in your hand, satisfy yourself with it. Don't put it down and go chasing after seven birds flying about in the sky.

Instead of concentrating on going to school, some people rather chase after visas to travel to Europe and America. I once knew a brilliant young man whom I personally encouraged to go to school, and even offered to pay his fees. But instead of going to school, he insisted that he would travel to America and make a lot of money there. For many years he sat around waiting for a visa to go to America. Ten years later, this young man who refused to go to school because he was waiting for a visa had graduated into an *adult illiterate*.

People are looking for something elsewhere, when there is something right before them. I know someone who became a millionaire just by taking photographs. He started out by taking photographs in my church, and became a millionaire.

There are things that are right before our eyes, yet we don't want them. We prefer something else. When God blesses you with something, use it!

I have loved my humble church in Ghana for many years. I believe this is what God has given to me. I am not going to go around chasing after fantasies. Develop the ground that lies before you and God will bless you through it.

I intend to till the ground that is before me and I know I will be blessed through it. But if I leave what is in my hands and go chasing after the wind, trying to become famous, I will have poverty enough!

6. **"He that hath" does not waste the blessings that come from the church. He that hath not is a waster of the blessings that come from the church.**

> For a day in thy courts is better than a thousand. I had rather be a doorkeeper in the house of my God, than to dwell in the tents of wickedness.
>
> Psalms 84:10

A good Christian must be able to faithfully stay in one church where he will receive nourishment. Many Christians waste the good churches and pastors that God gives to them and thereby become poor. When they hear of a new church, they flock there. These are the immature Christians attracted by flashy and showy things. "That we henceforth be no more children, tossed to and fro, and carried about with every wind of doctrine, by the sleight of men, and cunning craftiness, whereby they lie in wait to deceive" (Ephesians 4:14).

7. **"He that hath" does not waste the blessings of the Word of God. He that hath not is a waster of the Word of God.**

How sweet are thy words unto my taste! yea, sweeter than honey to my mouth!

Psalms 119:103

Neither have I gone back from the commandment of his lips; I have esteemed the words of his mouth more than my necessary food.

Job 23: 12

8. **"He that hath" does not waste the opportunity to receive wisdom from nature and God's creation.**

He that hath not has an almost standard response to wisdom when it is presented. They say it is not possible, they say it is not practical and they say it has never been done before. Wisdom is only useful when it is used. Wisdom makes you rich when you apply it practically in a real way. "Happy is the man that findeth wisdom, and the man that getteth understanding. For the merchandise of it is better than the merchandise of silver, and the gain thereof than fine gold. She is more precious than rubies: and all the things thou canst desire are not to be compared unto her. Length of days is in her right hand; and in her left hand riches and honour" (Proverbs 3:13-16).

When the opportunity comes to apply the wisdom of God many Christians make fun of it. When you suggest to people to study nature and learn the wisdom of the animals that God has created, they laugh at you. Have you ever wondered why some people love nature and wild life? There are so many things to learn from the things that God has created. Even the nature of God can be learnt by studying the things that God has created. "For since the creation of the world His invisible attributes, His eternal power and divine nature, have been clearly seen, being understood through what has been made, so that they are without excuse" (Romans 1:20, NASB).

For example, studying ants can give great wisdom to the simple. King Solomon studied animals and it made him wise.

He spoke three thousand proverbs and his songs numbered a thousand and five.

He described plant life, from the cedar of Lebanon to the hyssop that grows out of walls. HE ALSO TAUGHT ABOUT ANIMALS AND BIRDS, REPTILES AND FISH.

Men of all nations came to listen to Solomon's wisdom, sent by all the kings of the world, who had heard of his wisdom.

1 Kings 4:32-34 (NIV)

We have the opportunity to learn from ants who work without supervision. People who do not have this wisdom have to be supervised constantly because it is dangerous to leave them unsupervised.

Go to the ant, thou sluggard; consider her ways, and be wise: Which having no guide, overseer, or ruler, Provideth her meat in the summer, *and* gathereth her food in the harvest.

How long wilt thou sleep, O sluggard? when wilt thou arise out of thy sleep?

Proverbs 6:6-9

If you are the type of worker who needs no supervision, you demonstrate that you have the wisdom of an ant. You also demonstrate that you are not wasting the opportunity to use this wisdom of the ant.

If your employer needs to employ someone to supervise you, then your supervisor will have to be paid the extra money that could have been given to you. Remember also that your supervisor will have to be paid more than you are paid.

When you need supervision, your value is less because you are further down in the hierarchy of the organisation.

I watched a documentary of an American airline which crashed somewhere in South America. It was a Boeing 757 with about 195 people on board. The co-pilot was the one flying the plane, and not the captain. One survivor recounted that he heard the co-pilot saying, "We are approaching the airport. The weather is very good, visibility is clear, and we expect to land shortly."

Suddenly, they heard a loud bang and the lights went out. This survivor woke up later on in the hospital. Just after the passengers had been assured of arriving safely, a terrible accident occurred and almost everybody was killed. There were only four survivors!

The recorded conversation between the captain and the co-pilot was revealing. The co-pilot was terribly lost. He had flown the plane completely off course and straight into a high mountain.

Unfortunately, this co-pilot was somebody who needed to be supervised constantly in order to avoid killing many people. And that is exactly what he did when he was not supervised. If the captain himself had been flying the plane, it might have been a different story.

I know some private businessmen in my church. If I were to go to their offices at eleven o'clock in the night, they would probably be there. At midnight on Sundays, some of them may be found in their offices working. Nobody tells them to work; neither does anyone admonish them to rise up early to go to work.

I know people who started out as drivers, but have risen to become managers because they needed no supervision. If you are reliable enough to work without supervision, you will rise. Do not waste the opportunity to use the wisdom that comes to you through nature.

9. "He that hath" does not waste the opportunity to win souls. He that hath not is a waster of the opportunity to win souls.

> For what is a man profited, if he shall gain the whole world, and lose his own soul? Or what shall a man give in exchange for his soul?
>
> Matthew 16:26

Why would I give up my profession as a medical doctor to become a minister of the Word? Do I not think that it is important to attend to the physical bodies of people? I do!

However, my Bible also tells me that the souls of men are more important than their physical bodies. "...what shall a man give in exchange for his soul?" A soul is more valuable than all the cities of London, New York, Paris, Copenhagen, Lagos, Nairobi, Johannesburg and Accra.

If I lose my opportunity to win souls now that I am on this earth I will regret it for the rest of eternity. If I win souls today, I am doing the most valuable thing on earth.

10. **"He that hath" does not waste the blessing of pastors and prophets sent to him by God. He that hath not is a waster of the blessings that come through pastors.**

And we beseech you, brethren, to KNOW THEM WHICH LABOUR AMONG YOU, and are over you in the Lord, and admonish you;

And to esteem them very highly in love for their work's sake. And be at peace among yourselves.

1 Thessalonians 5:12-13

Many people do not know the great value of the humble pastors that minister to them every Sunday. You sometimes wonder what such church members are looking for. Whenever they hear that a powerful prophet is working wonders somewhere else, they jump on the bandwagon. Many people follow one sensational prophet after another, never being satisfied with their pastor, people subject themselves to all kinds of tricksters who swindle them of their money and destroy their lives.

Instead of honouring their pastors, church members would rather honour a sensational visiting minister with amazing offerings and gifts. They are so impressed with new and spectacular things. This is because they do not know the value of the pastor who regularly cares for them and speaks into their lives. Because they do not honour the right person, they do not receive the complete blessing and impartation that they could have from their pastors.

11. "He that hath" does not waste the opportunities that God gives to him. He that hath not is a waster of the opportunities that God gives to him.

In Luke 7:36, we read about the Pharisee who asked Jesus to dinner. In the course of the meal, a woman showed up with an alabaster bottle of ointment and poured it on His feet.

Then she began to wash His feet with her tears and to wipe them with her hair, kissing and anointing them with the ointment.

When the Pharisee saw that Jesus did not stop the woman, he began to question Jesus' credibility as a prophet. To him, Jesus could not discern that the woman was a sinner.

Jesus discerned the heart of the Pharisee and gave a parable to explain that the woman had shown great appreciation to Him for His ministry.

> **...I entered into thine house, thou gavest me no water for my feet: but she hath washed my feet with tears, and wiped them with the hairs of her head. Thou gavest me no kiss: but this woman since the time I came in hath not ceased to kiss my feet.**

> **Luke 7:44, 45**

This was a woman who felt Jesus was so important that while Jesus was alive, she anointed His feet with the most expensive perfume and wiped them with her hair.

It is interesting to note that when Jesus died, the women who had worked with Him came with prepared spices and ointments to anoint Him.

But it was too late! They met two people dressed in white like angels, who told them that He had risen from the grave.

Now upon the first day of the week, very early in the morning, they came unto the sepulchre, bringing the spices...And they found the stone rolled away...they were much perplexed...

Luke 24:1, 2, 4

You will be equally bewildered when you discover too late that something valuable has been taken away from you. The opportunity is gone forever! These women came with all their valuable ointments to anoint the Master, but it was too late. When Jesus was with them, they probably did not realize how valuable He was.

Many people don't realize the importance of something until it is gone. All over the world, people are hailed after their death.

The first president of Ghana, Kwame Nkrumah, was insulted, ridiculed and exiled when he was alive. Many years after his death, some political parties struggled to identify with him, calling themselves "Nkrumahists".

Many great people are recognized and valued after they are gone. When my father died I wept like a baby. Suddenly, I realized his value in a way I had never known when he was alive! When you lose something forever, you realize how valuable it has been to your existence.

During the funeral of Ron Brown (the American Secretary of Commerce, who died in a plane crash), his son read his tribute which was carried live by CNN. He said something which struck me as underlining the principle of timely valuation.

I think he said something to this effect: "I have no feelings of regret. I have said all that I could have said to him. There is nothing that I could have said which I didn't say. I have had the best of relationships with my father. On the day that he travelled I kissed him goodbye on his lips."

This was a son who probably had little to regret after he lost his father. Little did he know that this would be his last opportunity to appreciate his father.

We need to value people and things before we lose them. Many are those who kneel at their parents' graves weeping. They grieve not only because the person is dead, but also because they didn't show appreciation to the person when he was alive. I urge you to look into your life and see whether there is anybody you need to value.

Hopefully, it is not too late to make amends - locate all such people and find a suitable way of expressing appreciation to them.

God is saying to His people that there are many things He has given us that often go waste. If you keep on wasting them, He will take them away from you. If God gives you a pastor and you don't value him, He will take him away from you. If God gives you a mother and you are not grateful for her, He will take her away. If God gives you money and resources to be a blessing to the house of God, and you fail to use it for that purpose, He will take it away and give it to someone else.

12.   "He that hath" does not waste the good seasons of life. He that hath not is a waster of the good seasons of his life.

Pharaoh had a dream about seven fat cows and seven lean ones. In the dream, he saw seven fat cows come out to graze. Suddenly, seven other extremely lean ones came out of the water and ate up the fat cows (Genesis 41:1-4).

Joseph, who was then a prisoner, explained to the King that the seven lean cows stood for years of poverty and the seven fat cows, for years of prosperity.

God advised Pharaoh through Joseph to store food during the times of plenty, so that he and the whole of Egypt would survive the lean years. This is wisdom from God.

Everybody's life has seven "lean cows" and seven "fat cows". The days of the seven fat cows will come, and so will the days of the seven lean cows.

There are always going to be seven lean cows and seven fat cows, and the lean ones will always eat the fat ones.

That means that there is a period when things will be good. So make the most of it by storing up for the "rainy day". If you save in those years, when the lean years come, you won't go-a-begging. The seven lean cows always eat up the seven fat ones, so if you are not wise during your prosperous season the lean season will be a horror to you.

Many old men look like they never had any wealth. It is possible that many of them did not take advantage of their seven fat cows.

My father was a very good lawyer, who handled many cases in court for several years. Through his hard work, he became rich and famous - those were his fat cow years. Later, he was taken seriously ill, and kept going in and out of hospital. But he had other investments which he reaped from in his later years.

If you do not learn to save and invest during your fat cow years, the lean cow years will suddenly overtake you, leaving you with nothing but faint memories of the past.

Other Books by Dag Heward-Mills

LOYALTY SERIES

Fathers and Loyalty

Leaders and Loyalty

Loyalty and Disloyalty

Those Who Accuse You

Those Who Forget

Those Who Leave You

Those Who Pretend

CHURCH BUILDING SERIES

Church Growth

Church Planting

The Mega Church (2nd Ed.)

ANOINTING SERIES

Catch the Anointing

Ministering with Signs and Wonders

Steps to the Anointing

WORK OF MINISTRY SERIES

How You Can Be in the Perfect Will of God

Losing, Suffering, Sacrificing, Dying

Many are Called

Proton

Rules of Church Work

Rules of Full-Time Ministry

The Art of Following

PASTORAL MINISTRY SERIES

The Art of Leadership (2nd Ed.)

The Art of Shepherding

Transform Your Pastoral Ministry

SUCCESS SERIES

Why Non-Tithing Christians Become Poor and How Tithing Christians Can Become Rich

He That Hath, to Him Shall Be Given: and He That Hath Not, from Him Shall Be Taken Even That Which He Hath.

CHRISTIAN LIFE SERIES

Backsliding

Daughter, You Can Make It

Demons and How to Deal with Them

Model Marriage

Name it! Claim it! Take it!

Quiet Time

Tell Them